A Walk Down Edinburgh's Royal Mile

Eric Melvin

Copyright © 2014 Eric Melvin

All rights reserved.

The right of Eric Melvin to be identified as the Author of the Work has been asserted by him in accordance with the Copyright, Designs and Patent Act 1988.

All rights reserved. No part of this publication may be reproduced, stored in a retrieval system, or transmitted, in any form or by any means without the prior written permission of the author and copyright owner, nor be otherwise circulated in any form of binding, or cover other than that in which it is published and without a similar condition being imposed on the subsequent purchaser.

ISBN: 1499518064

ISBN-13: 978 – 1499518061

DEDICATION & THANKS

I would like to express my sincere thanks to Alison Stoddart of the City of Edinburgh Council City Libraries Department for her help in identifying photographs from the excellent Capital Collections.

I am also grateful to Peter Stubbs of Edinburgh Photos for allowing me to include images from his on-line collection.

I am very much indebted to my brother Alan Melvin who has produced the maps to guide the reader through each section of the walk. He has also deployed his considerable editorial skills over the text to great advantage.

Finally a sincere 'thank you' to my cousin Lesley Winton for her help and expertise in taking this project forward and to my dear wife, Lynda Melvin for her invaluable 'critical eye' and encouragement.

This book is dedicated to my son John Melvin

CONTENTS

1. *Introduction ps. 1 - 5*

2. *The Castlehill ps. 6 - 14*

3. *The Lawnmarket ps. 15 - 30*

4. *The High Street ps. 31 – 71*

5. *The Canongate ps. 72 – 103*

   Index ps. 104 -110

Illustration Credits

With the kind permission of the City of Edinburgh Council – Libraries.
www.capitalcollections.org.uk
ps. 13, 14, 35 (top), 39, 40 (top), 41, 42, 43, 47, 49, 50, 57, 59, 71 (top), 72, 76, 77, 78, 102.

Eric Melvin
eric.melvin@btinternet.com
ps. 1, 4, 6, 8, 9, 10, 11, 12, 15, 18, 20, 22, 24, 25, 26, 27, 29, 30, 31, 34, 35 (bottom), 37, 38, 40 (bottom), 45, 48, 51, 52, 53, 54, 55, 56, 58, 60, 61, 62, 63, 65, 66, 68, 69, 70, 71 (bottom), 74, 75, 79, 80, 81, 82, 83, 84, 85, 86, 87, 88, 89, 90, 91, 92, 94, 96, 98, 100, 101, 103.

Reproduced with grateful acknowledgement to Peter Stubbs of Edinburgh Photos.
peter.stubbs@edinphotoorg.uk
ps. 3, 5.

Maps on ps. 7, 16, 32 & 73 drawn by Alan Melvin.

1. INTRODUCTION

Edinburgh Castle

Edinburgh's Royal Mile is one of the most famous streets in the world. For well over a thousand years, the street has been at the heart of Scotland's capital city. Why the Royal Mile? Well our journey is going to take us down this ancient street from a Royal Castle to a Royal Palace. You are going to be following in the footsteps of many famous Scots including King Robert Bruce, King James IV, Mary, Queen of Scots and our country's national poet, Robert Burns.

Just take a look at Edinburgh Castle before you. This is without doubt one of the most famous buildings in the world. For over 1000 years, Edinburgh Castle has been right at the heart of Scotland's History. It is Scotland's most popular paying tourist attraction with over 1.3 million visitors each year. The Castle, steeped in history and home to the Crown Jewels of Scotland, is a 'must' for any visitors to the City.

Now, before we start just a brief word about how Edinburgh has been shaped by geology and history. Some 350 million years ago, where you are standing was under an ocean pierced by active volcanoes. The well-known Arthur's Seat was at one time one of these volcanoes. Then as recently as 12000 years ago the whole of Scotland, and indeed northern Europe, was covered by an enormous, slow-moving mountain of ice during the last Ice Age. This huge glacier ground down mountains and gouged out valleys. The valleys of Princes Street Gardens to your right and the Grassmarket below you on your left are examples of that. The Castle Rock though, being hard volcanic rock survived but the softer rocks and earth were carried away to form the foundations for what is now the Royal Mile. Edinburgh grew on top of this glacial debris.

Where does the name *'Edinburgh'* come from? Until the 7th century, the settlement on that Castle Rock was known as Dunedin – the fortified township on the steep hill. Dunedin was a fortified stronghold held by Celtic people, known to the Romans as the Votadini, who spoke Brythonic, a language like present-day Welsh. Then in the 600s, Dunedin was captured by an English army and for some 400 years this area of Scotland, known as Lothian, was part of the English kingdom of Northumbria. The occupying English replaced *'Dun'* with their word for a fortified settlement *'burgh'*, and so the name Edinburgh was born. Lothian was recaptured by the Scots in 1018. For centuries Scotland was a separate, independent kingdom. Often there was war with our powerful English neighbour. Scots can make the mistake of thinking that the War of Independence finished with Robert Bruce's victory over the English at Bannockburn in June 1314. In fact the fighting continued on and off for nearly 300 years. Being just a few days march from the English border, Edinburgh was often in the front line.

On several occasions, such as in 1385 and 1544, the town was seriously damaged by occupying English soldiers. But in 1603, King James VI of Scotland, born in Edinburgh Castle, succeeded his cousin Queen Elizabeth of England to become the first King of the new United Kingdom.

Edinburgh Castle about the year 1500

This is how the Castle looked about the year 1500. There was no Esplanade and the approach was heavily defended. The Royal Apartments to the left have survived but the tall tower in the centre, King David's Tower, was destroyed in the great siege of 1573 when the Castle was seized from supporters of the imprisoned Mary, Queen of Scots.

The famous Half-Moon Battery was built after the siege on the ruins of King David's Tower. The Esplanade was laid out in the 1750s and became a popular place for Edinburgh folk to stroll and to meet with their friends.

Each August the Esplanade is the venue for the world-famous Edinburgh Military Tattoo, one of the highlights of the Edinburgh International Festival. The first Tattoo was held here in 1950. Thousands of spectators from all over the world enjoy displays of marching, music, singing and dancing. The highlight is the thrilling sight of the massed pipes and drums marching through the Castle gates.

The Edinburgh Festival Military Tattoo

The Royal Mile lies at the heart of what is known as The Old Town of Edinburgh. It has four separate sections running from west to east. At the foot of the Esplanade is the Castlehill. We then have the Lawnmarket which runs from the top of the West Bow to George IV Bridge. The High Street carries on from there to the Netherbow Port, beside John Knox's House. Finally we have the Canongate which until 1864 was a separate burgh. The Canongate takes us to the Scottish Parliament building and finally to Holyrood Palace.

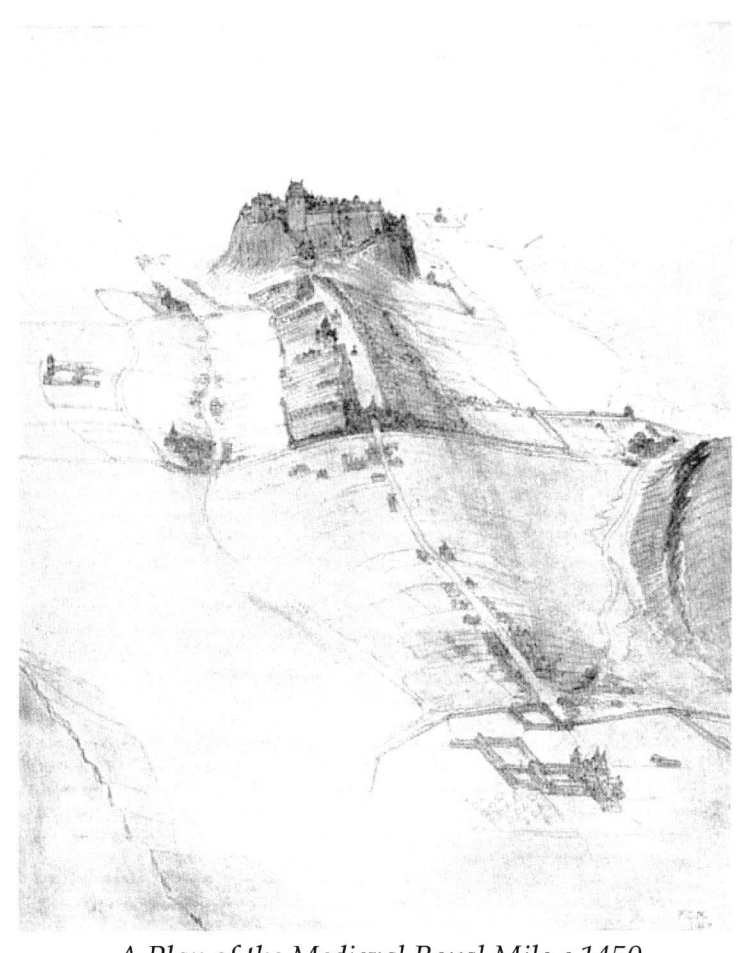

A Plan of the Medieval Royal Mile c 1450

This artist's reconstruction of The Royal Mile about the year 1500 shows the long street fronted by the houses of wealthy merchants known as burgesses. Edinburgh is protected by the King's Wall, and by the Nor' Loch. Edinburgh ends partway down the Royal Mile and the Netherbow Port (a protected gateway), separates Edinburgh from the Canongate. At the foot of the Royal Mile is the wealthy Holyrood Abbey. Beyond the wall on the left (to the south) are the monasteries of the Greyfriars and the Blackfriars.

2. THE CASTLEHILL

Cannonball House and the top of the Castlehill

MAP 1

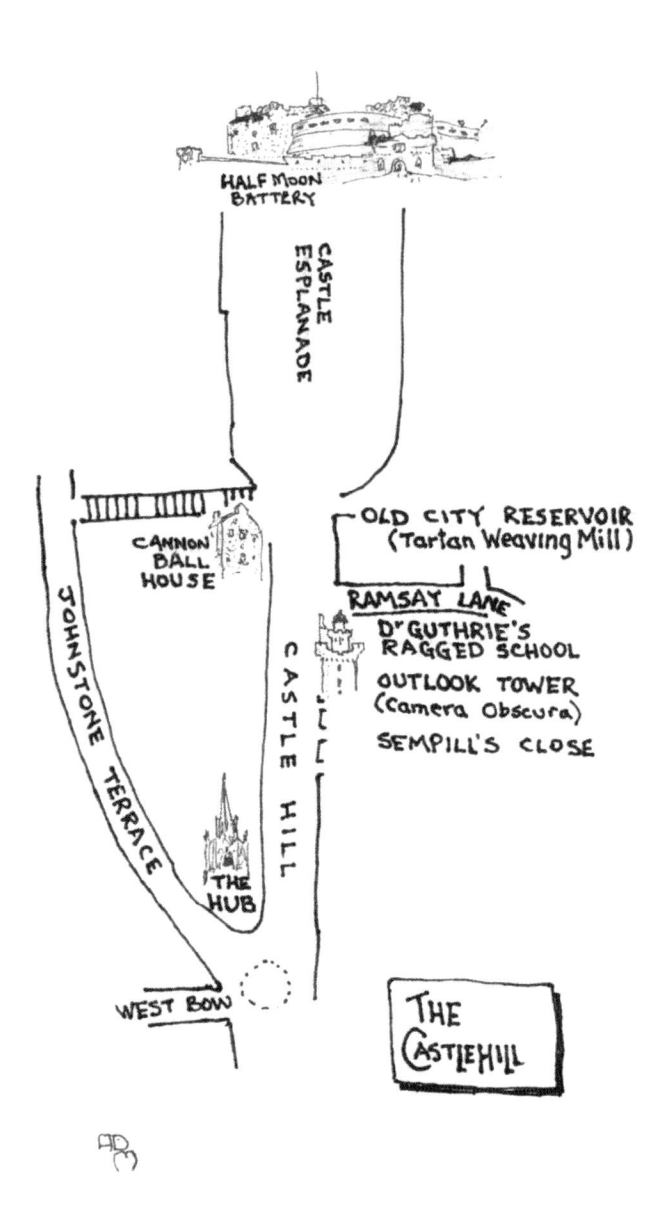

HALF MOON BATTERY

CASTLE ESPLANADE

OLD CITY RESERVOIR (Tartan Weaving Mill)

CANNON BALL HOUSE

RAMSAY LANE

Dr GUTHRIE'S RAGGED SCHOOL

OUTLOOK TOWER (Camera Obscura)

SEMPILL'S CLOSE

JOHNSTONE TERRACE

CASTLE HILL

THE HUB

WEST BOW

THE CASTLEHILL

Cannonball House

Immediately on your right beside a steep flight of steps is a surviving 17th century house. Go down a few of the steps and look at the small, pointed dormer window at the top of the house above you on your left. You should be able to make out the letters AM and MN. These are the initials of Alexander Mure and his wife, Margaret Neillans along with the date 1630. This was the year of their wedding when they moved into this house. As you can see, the stone work looks pretty rough and ready. It's a style known as 'rubble built' where the builders just cemented undressed stones together rather than neatly cutting them to shape.

When you see houses like this in Edinburgh then you will know that they are usually at least 250 years old.

The initials of Alexander Mure and Margaret Neillans

The house is known as *'Cannonball House'*. If you look closely above the first floor window on your left, you'll see a cannonball. Look further along and there is another damaged one stuck into the stonework. So what's the story?
If you'd been standing here in September 1745 then you would have been ducking for cover. Here was the siege line of a Jacobite *(Latin for the followers of James)* army trying to capture Edinburgh Castle. You may have heard of Bonnie Prince Charlie? He was trying to regain the throne for his exiled father James Stuart.

Charlie had captured Edinburgh and was determined to capture the Castle as well. However the Castle Governor had other ideas! The 87 year old General Preston bombarded the town. For two days his cannon did terrible damage, including smashing down the walls of the house in front of you. To save further destruction, Charlie called off the siege. The Jacobite army left Edinburgh at the end of October and marched south towards London. They reached Derby just 200 kms from the capital. With little support and with government forces threatening, the fateful decision was taken on December 5th to retreat back to Scotland. Prince Charlie's dream of regaining the throne for his father was destroyed outside Inverness at the bloody battle of Culloden fought on April 16th, 1746.

As for Cannonball House, it is thought that the builders, brought in to repair the damage, cemented in these two cannonballs as souvenirs of the last siege of Edinburgh Castle.

One of the two cannonballs of Cannonball House

Now make your way down the Castlehill. The building immediately on your left used to be the City Reservoir. The first reservoir was built here in 1675 to carry water to several public wells some of which are still to be seen on the Royal Mile and in the Grassmarket. This building dates from 1851 and held 1.7 million gallons of water.

This next building on your left was started in 1847 as *'A Ragged School.'* This was the inspiration of Doctor Thomas Guthrie, a minister of the Free Church of Scotland whose church was nearby. He was appalled by the sight of so many poor children crowding the closes and wynds of the Royal Mile and struggling to survive amidst the dirt, poverty and crime of the mid - 19th century Old Town. In the first years of 'The Ragged School' over 500 children were rescued from the streets. The condition of these children was truly shocking. Dr. Guthrie found that 140 had no father while 89 had no mother. He further recorded that of these 66 were motherless with drunken fathers while 77 were fatherless with drunken mothers. Many had simply been abandoned by their parents, with 271 reduced to begging.

Dr. Guthrie's 'Ragged School'

Ninety-five of them had been arrested by the Police for stealing and some had even spent time in prison. These children were cleaned, fed, clothed and given a basic education in the hope that they could earn a decent living and escape from poverty. There is statue of Dr. Guthrie in Princes Street Gardens.

Beside 'The Ragged School' is The Outlook Tower. It is built around an old 17th century mansion house. In 1846 the house was converted into an observatory by Maria Short. She installed a Camera Obscura which still delights visitors with its panoramic views of the City.

The Outlook Tower

In 1891 the property was bought by Professor Sir Patrick Geddes and converted into *'The Outlook Tower.'* This was a new-style visitor centre which encouraged people to *"think global; act local."* By this Geddes meant that we all have a responsibility to look after our environment. Geddes is seen today as an expert in town planning and one of the first to champion conservation and the care of the environment.

While working at the University of Edinburgh, he purchased several older properties in the Royal Mile, which were threatened with demolition, and in partnership with Edinburgh Council and others sympathetic to his vision, helped to restore them. Thanks to Patrick Geddes, these surviving buildings such as Lady Stair's House, White Horse Close and James Court can still be enjoyed by visitors today.

There is a *'Patrick Geddes Trail'* that takes you through the Old Town which highlights some of the old buildings that he managed to conserve and to restore.

Professor Sir Patrick Geddes

A few metres further down on your left, you will come to Sempill's Close. Here you will find the townhouse of the Sempill family. The house dates from 1638. This house is a reminder that when the Scottish Royal Court came to Edinburgh or when the Scottish Parliament, known as the Three Estates, was meeting here, then the most powerful families in the land would come to stay in the capital. Several had town houses such as this one built for themselves. You can see that the approach down a narrow, twisting flight of stairs is rather awkward. This was deliberate and was built like this to help defend the house in troubled times. Above one of the doors is the motto *'Praise be the Lord, My God, My Strength and My Redeemer.'* In April 1746 the 12th Lord Sempill commanded a regiment on the left wing of the Government army which defeated Bonnie Prince Charlie's Jacobite forces at the Battle of Culloden.

Moving down the Castlehill, the church building on your right was built between 1842 and 1845. The architect was J. Gillespie Graham. Its impressive Gothic spire is the tallest in Edinburgh. The building is now known as The Hub and is the Headquarters of the Edinburgh International Festival. Beyond the Hub and running to the right is Johnstone Terrace. This dates from 1828 and was built to improve access into and out of the Old Town. Several old buildings had to be knocked down for this road to be built.

Among these was *'The Stripping Close'*. Here men and women who had been sentenced to be whipped as a punishment for their crimes, were stripped to the waist before being whipped through the Old Town by the burgh's public executioner. The last public whipping took place in 1822. This street is named after Sir William Johnston who was Lord Provost in 1848. With his brother Alexander, Sir William founded the well-known Edinburgh map-making business W & A. K. Johnstone in 1826.

Castlehill in the 1850s

3. THE LAWNMARKET

The top of the West Bow on the Lawnmarket

MAP 2

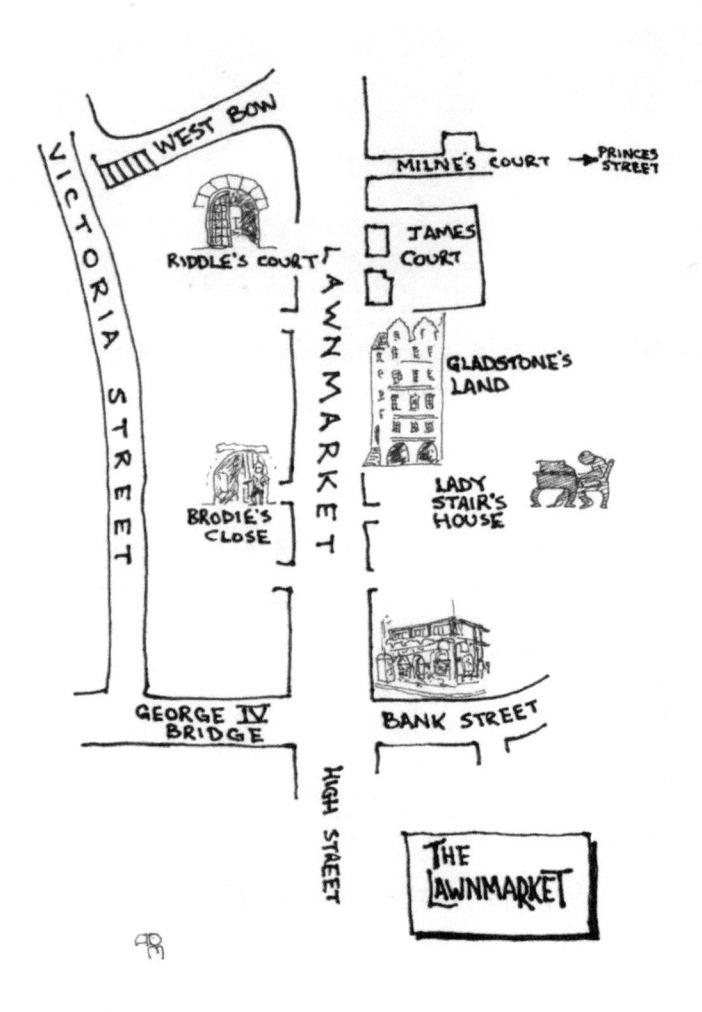

The Lawnmarket has a long history. A Charter of King James III, granted in 1477 allowed a Cloth Market to be started here. To your right is one of the original entrances into the Old Town. This was known as The West Bow. This was a steep twisting road that led up from the Grassmarket to the south.

Make your way down the West Bow to the top of a steep flight of steps leading up from Victoria Street below you. Move forward to the railings and look down to your right towards the oldest part of the street. There are two of the original houses just at the bend, one them rubble-built like Cannonball House. Until the early 1800s, the main approach to Edinburgh from the north and the west was up this steep winding street. There were no steps in those days, so the last stretch up to the Royal Mile must have been very tough going. Just imagine all the famous visitors who must have passed by where you are standing! These included Robert Burns who clattered up here on a borrowed horse on the evening of 28th November 1786. This was the first of several visits that the poet made to Edinburgh. Encouraged by his friends, he came here to seek support for the publication of a second edition of his poems.

There were others who came this way as well. This was the route taken over the years by hundreds of condemned criminals who were led past here from the Tollbooth, the town gaol, to be executed in the Grassmarket down to your right at the foot of the West Bow. One of the most infamous prisoners to be dragged down here was the accused witch Grizel Weir. Edinburgh has the reputation for being one of the most haunted cities in the world. There are two ghosts said to haunt the area beside you – Grizel and her brother, the alleged warlock (a male witch) Major Thomas Weir.

At the top of West Bow

Major Thomas Weir lived just near where you are standing at the top of the West Bow with his sister who went by the unusual old Scots' name of Grizel. Major Weir was born in 1600 and had had a distinguished military career fighting in the Scottish Covenanting army during the English Civil Wars. In those deeply-religious days, Weir stood out as a man of great devotion. He held regular prayer meetings in his house and was known locally as 'Angelical Thomas'. He was often attended by a group of young women who, with Thomas and Grizel Weir, were known as *'The Bowhead Saints'*.

Weir had a striking appearance. He was tall with a grim-looking face and a long pointed nose. He usually wore a long black cape and a wide-brimmed black hat. He was always seen carrying a walking stick. However there was a much darker side to him.

In 1670 Weir took ill and thought that he was dying. He sent for the Provost, Sir Andrew Ramsay. You can imagine the shock for Sir Andrew when instead of quiet prayers shared together, the sick man poured out a confession of wickedness. The Provost was so appalled that Weir was immediately arrested and carried on his sick-bed to the town jail, the Tollbooth. There he raved about having sold his soul to the Devil and committing all manner of revolting crimes. He was tried as a warlock and sentenced to death. When asked to pray for forgiveness he screamed:

"Torment me no more – I am tortured enough already. As I am going to the Devil anyway I do not wish to anger him!"

This was a very superstitious age. People were terrified at the thought of witchcraft and evil-doing. So Weir was taken outside Edinburgh to a spot half-way down the present-day Leith Walk for his execution. He was first strangled and then burnt at the stake in front of a huge crowd of terrified onlookers. An old Edinburgh tradition was that his stick screamed when it was thrown into the flames.

Then it was the turn of his sister. Poor Grizel was tortured and confessed to being a witch. She was taken down the West Bow past her house where you are standing and hanged in front of a huge crowd in the Grassmarket. For years after the house was looked upon with dread. Local folk were convinced that any clatter of hooves late at night was the Devil on his black horse searching for his old companions. No-one could stay long in the Weirs' house. It was considered as haunted and was finally demolished in 1878.

From a ghost story we now must consider a murder. Walk back up to the top of the Lawnmarket and turn right down the south side of the street, then enter Riddle's Court.

Riddle's Court and Baillie McMorran's House

Now walk through the 18th century courtyard to the metal gate ahead of you. Notice the corbelled stone work above you to your left. This is how the street frontage would have looked in the late 1500s. A wealthy merchant, known as a burgess, would have had his home and his business premises fronting onto the Royal Mile with a garden or perhaps other property behind. This property was protected by an iron gate like the one in front of you. This would be shut at night for security. This closing of the gate gives us the name *'Close'* which is to be found attached to many of the narrow streets running off the Royal Mile. Riddle's Court is named after an early 18th century Edinburgh burgess who lived here. The Close is well-known for two incidents in the 1590s – a banquet and a violent death.

In 1598 King James VI (soon to become King James I of England) accompanied by his Danish wife Queen Anne were entertained by the Burgh to a banquet in the house at the rear of the Court beyond the metal barrier.

The host to the royal couple was the owner of the property, the rich merchant, Baillie William McMorran. (A Baillie was a senior member of the Town Council).

In 1595, this house was lived in by William's brother, Baillie James McMorran. He too was a rich merchant and one of Edinburgh's senior councillors. Much is made today about the bad behaviour of school pupils. It seems that things were even worse in the 16th century. In September 1595 the boys of the High School went on strike and locked themselves into the school. Their behaviour had been so bad that the Headteacher, who went by the wonderful name of Hercules Rollock, cancelled the September school holiday. The boys defied all attempts to persuade them to open the door, so word was sent to Baillie McMorran to come to persuade the boys to stop the protest.

No doubt grumbling about his interrupted breakfast, Baillie McMorran agreed. Imagine then the Baillie in his magnificent robes and chain of office sweeping out through this Court to the Lawnmarket. Followed by a growing crowd of curious onlookers, he made his way to the school situated then at the foot of Blackfriars Wynd further down the High Street. He approached the door and demanded that the boys surrender themselves. At that, a hand appeared from a first floor window; a hand with a pistol. A shot was fired and poor Baillie McMorran dropped down dead. In panic, the boys fled from the scene of the crime as best they could. Some jumped out of windows, while others even climbed up the chimneys. The murderer though was caught. He was William Sinclair, aged just ten, the son of the Chancellor of Caithness, one of the most powerful men in Scotland. Because of his age and his connections he was never brought to trial. Indeed his descendants were to become the Earls of Caithness. There was no justice for poor Baillie McMorran.

This historic Close is one of those rescued by Sir Patrick Geddes, who was knighted in 1932 just before his death in France where he had retired to the town of Montpellier. He renovated Riddle's Court and refurbished Baillie McMorran's house converting it into Halls of Residence for the University of Edinburgh for women undergraduates.

Now return to the Lawnmarket and move slightly further down to the entrance of Brodie's Close,

Deacon William Brodie (in black) and George Smith

Notice again the metal gate at the entrance to the Close. This was the home of the notorious Deacon William Brodie who was hanged in October 1788 in front of St Giles Kirk just ahead of you further down the High Street.

To most Edinburgh folk of his day Deacon Brodie was an upright citizen and a successful tradesman, being the Deacon or head of the Society of Cabinetmakers. He had inherited a very prosperous business from his father, Francis Brodie. Like his father, Deacon Brodie was a member of the Town Council He was a familiar figure striding down the Royal Mile to visit his workmen clad in his silver-buckled shoes, smart breeches, jacket, fancy waistcoat and fashionable tricorn hat.

There was though another Deacon Brodie, known to only a few. While he might have appeared the respectable citizen by day, at night he lived a very different life. For Brodie was a heavy drinker, a womaniser with two mistresses and above all a serious gambler who regularly could be found playing cards and dice or frequenting the hugely popular cockfights. Inevitably this riotous lifestyle saw Brodie get seriously into debt. It is a sobering thought that in the 18th century you could be imprisoned for debt. How different from today with our plastic credit cards! What was Brodie to do to avoid public shame and humiliation?

To save his reputation Brodie turned to burglary. He was remarkably clever. When he visited his workmen, he would take a lump of putty in his hand and when no-one was looking, he would make an impression of the house keys which were often left hanging from a hook behind the front door. So Brodie was able to slip in and out of the houses that he burgled without leaving any sign of a forced entry. Brodie though got greedy. With three others, Andrew Ainslie, John Brown and George Smith, he planned a robbery of the Excise Office in Chessel's Court, just further down the Royal Mile. The robbers though were disturbed by a clerk, Andrew Bonar, who had returned for some papers.

They fled but Ainslie and Brown were quickly arrested and turned King's Evidence to save their lives as burglary then was a hanging offence. Brodie fled south to London hotly pursued by the law. Using a variety of disguises and aliases, he disappeared. The trail went cold and he would have escaped justice if he had not sent some letters to friends and to his mistress. The hunt was on again.

Brodie was arrested in Amsterdam on the point of boarding ship for New York. He was brought back to Edinburgh, put on trial and along with George Smith, sentenced to be hanged. By a curious twist of fate, Brodie and Smith were to be executed on a new scaffold with a trapdoor that Brodie had reputedly designed himself. A huge crowd had gathered. Brodie appeared as smartly dressed as ever. There was a fault though with the scaffold. Unperturbed Brodie talked with his friends and sang from *'The Beggar's Opera'*, the hit musical of the day. At last the execution was carried out. Brodie was gone, but of course he became the inspiration for Edinburgh author Robert Louis Stevenson's *'Dr. Jekyll and Mr. Hyde'* published in 1886 – the dark tale of a good man by day and a monster at night.

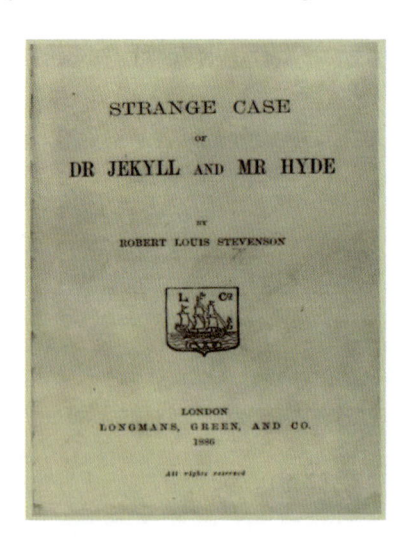

Across the road from where you are standing there is a building with a golden hawk as decoration. This is Gladstone's Land (*'Land'* meaning the property belonged to someone.) This is a fine example of a surviving merchant's house of the early 1600s. Thomas Gladstone was a cloth merchant and bought this property in 1617. He carried out his business underneath the arches in front of you at street level. The typical outside stone stair is one of the few left that we can still see. Gladstone's Land has been restored as a 17th century townhouse by the National Trust for Scotland and is well worth a visit.

Gladstone's Land

Now walk back up to Milne's Court just across from the top of the West Bow.

The Entrance to Milne's Court

Milne's Court was developed in 1690 by Robert Milne (or Mylne), the King's Royal Master Mason for Scotland. It was the first courtyard development in the Old Town. Its upmarket apartments proved very popular and encouraged several similar developments in the 18th century. By the middle of the 19th century though it had become a very rundown, overcrowded slum. The census of 1851 recorded 468 people living here. Again we have to thank Patrick Geddes for rescuing the Court. The west side was knocked down but Geddes campaigned successfully to save the remaining buildings. It was restored again in the 1960s and is now Halls of Residence for the University of Edinburgh.

Now move down to the neighbouring James' Court.

James Court

This is named after James Brownhill who built this open-court development between 1723 -1727. It became very much a *'des res'* for those Edinburgh citizens who could afford the high rents asked for. Amongst the well-known residents were David Hume and James Boswell. Those able to afford the high rents of James Court had to follow very strict regulations. In 1786 the 1st Regulation stated

"No person shall at any time throw out, from any window or door in the Court, any water, ashes, or nastiness of any kind…"

This was an attempt to stop the Edinburgh practice of people just tipping their waste and rubbish out of their tenement windows into the street below.

They would cry out *"Gardy-Loo!"* taken from the French meaning *"Watch out for the water!"* – though of course it wasn't just water being tipped out. The Council tried to stop this practice by threatening fines and even imprisonment but it was impossible to police. While folk were supposed to put their household waste out at 10.00 pm at night to be collected by scavengers, you can appreciate for those living several stories up a tenement, you were not going to climb down a dark, twisty, dirty stair to put out your waste and then climb back up again. So out of the windows it went. With some 60000 residents crowded then into the Old Town, the smell must have been simply dreadful. This awful smell together with the smoke from the hundreds of chimneys gave Edinburgh the nickname of *'Auld Reekie.'* Here's how an English visitor, Captain Edmund Burt, described a narrow escape that he had as he made his way home in 1734.

"When I first came into the High Street of that City I had not seen anything of the kind more magnificent, the extreme height of the houses; the breadth and length of the street. I was extremely pleased.

We supped very plentifully…and were very merry till the clock struck 10, the hour when everybody is at liberty…to throw their filth out at the windows. The company then began to light pieces of paper…to smoke the room and, as I thought, to mix one bad smell with another. (Having) to pass to my new lodgings, a guide was assigned to me, who went before me to prevent my disgrace…The opening of a window made me tremble, while behind and before me…fell the terrible shower."

Walk through Close and down the steps. Ahead of you is Lady Stair's House. This is a surviving townhouse of a member of the nobility, once fronted by a garden. It was built in 1622 by Sir William Gray. (If you look carefully you can see his initials and the date above the front door).

Lady Stair's House is now an interesting Writers' Museum celebrating some of Edinburgh's most famous authors. Like the three other City of Edinburgh Museums to be found on the Royal Mile, admission is free.

In the early 1700s this was the home of the beautiful widow Lady Primrose.

Lady Stair's House

The cruelty of her late husband had persuaded her not to remarry. However the celebrated Earl of Stair was determined to have her hand. She refused all his advances.

In desperation he bribed his way into her house and in the morning he stood at the street window with nothing on to give the impression that he and Lady Primrose were in a relationship. Poor Lady Primrose felt obliged to marry him to protect her reputation. At first it was a very unhappy marriage. The Earl of Stair, like many of his contemporaries, was a very heavy drinker. One night when drunk, he assaulted his wife. Although bruised and bleeding, Lady Stair did not have her injuries attended to. Instead she sat in her chair while her drunken husband slept. When the Earl awoke next morning he was so shocked to see what he had done, that he promised that in future he would only drink what she poured out for him. After that the couple enjoyed a long and happy life together. Lady Stair died in 1759. This property is another of those rescued by Patrick Geddes who persuaded Lord Rosebury, a descendent of Sir William Gray, to purchase the house and to gift it to the City.

Across the Close was the house where Robert Burns stayed on his first visit to Edinburgh in 1786.

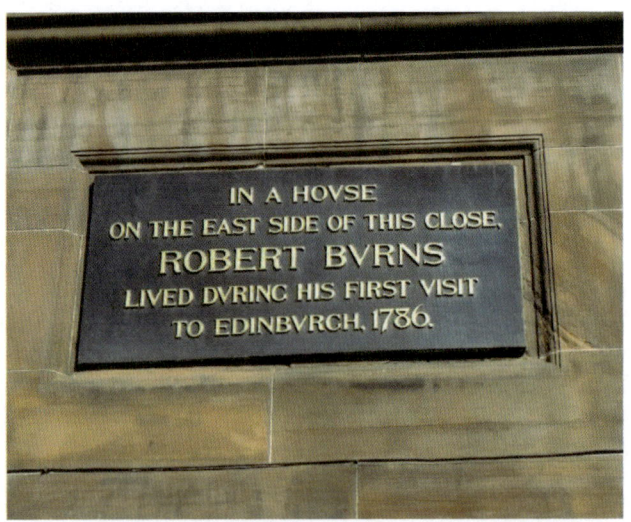

Commemorative Plaque on the Lawnmarket

4. THE HIGH STREET

The Old Mercat Cross in the High Street of Edinburgh

MAP 3

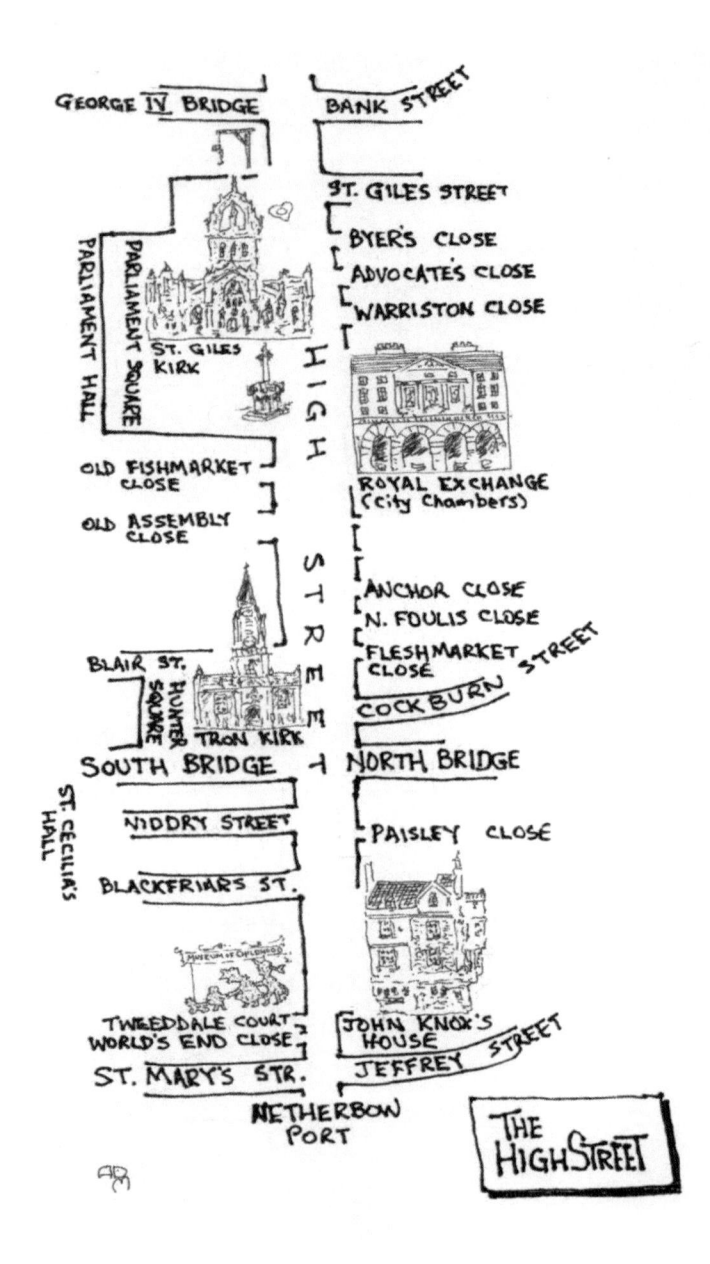

Cross over the road using the crossing lights. On your right is George IV Bridge. This was designed by Thomas Hamilton. It was built between 1827 – 1836 and was named in honour of King George IV who had visited the City in 1822. The bridge, designed by Thomas Hamilton, linked the Old Town with the spreading suburbs to the south. The bridge is some 275 metres long and has eight arches, only one of which is visible.

Its construction saw the destruction of many old properties including Old Bank Close, scene of the murder of Lord President of the Court of Session, Sir George Lockhart who was shot dead by John Chiesley of Dalry on his way home from church in March 1689. Chiesley had been angered by a decision against him made by the judge in favour of his estranged wife. Chiesley was arrested, He was quoted as saying

"I do not want to do things by halves and now I have taught the Lord President how to do justice."

Chiesley was tortured to see if he had any accomplices. His right hand was cut off and his pistol was hung round his neck. He was dragged from the Tollbooth to the Mercat Cross and hanged in chains.

Liberton's Wynd, home to Dowie's Tavern a favourite 18th pub, was also demolished to make way for the planned bridge. It was famous for its Edinburgh Ale which was described by a contemporary as:

"a potent fluid which almost glued the lips of the drinker together and of which therefore few could despatch more than a bottle."

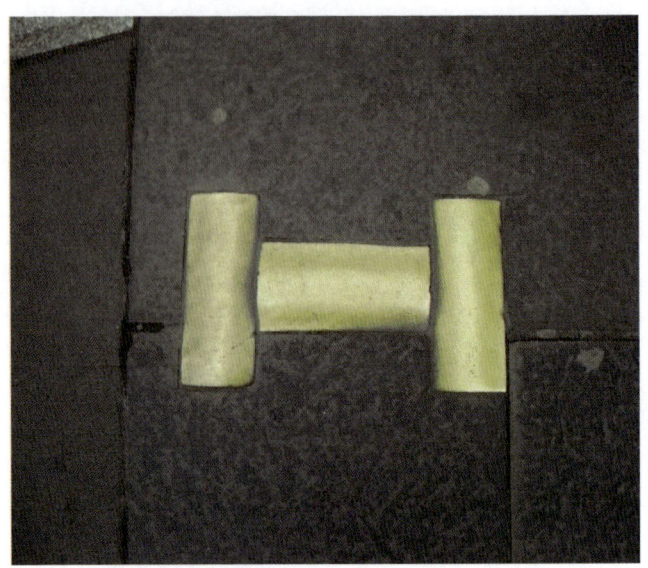

The site of the last public execution.

These brass setts at the corner of the High Street mark the site of the gallows used for the last public hanging that was carried out in Edinburgh. This was the execution of George Bryce, the *'Ratho Murderer.'* Bryce had killed his girlfriend in a fit of temper. He was hanged on the morning of 20th June 1864 before a crowd of between 20000 – 30000 jeering people. Bryce went to his death calmly muttering to himself *"keep composed; keep composed."* After this condemned criminals were hanged at the Calton Gaol completed in 1817.

This was also the spot where the notorious murderer William Burke was hanged in January 1829. Some 25000 watched his execution. You will learn more about his dreadful crimes later on in your Walk down the Royal Mile.

The Execution of William Burke - 1829

You are now standing at the start of the section of the Royal Mile known as the High Street.

The High Street of Edinburgh

As you walk down the left-hand (north) side of this part of the High Street you will pass three very old closes dating back to medieval times - Byers Close, Advocate's Close and Warriston Close. These steep, narrow alley-ways are typical of the ninety or so closes and wynds that once ran to the north and to the south off the Royal Mile. (Wynds were public rights of way). These were often named after famous citizens who lived there or they identified a trade that was located here in days gone by. Fishmarket Close a little further down on the south side of the High Street is such an example. Byers Close is named after John Byers of Coates (1569-1629) Lord Provost of Edinburgh and City Treasurer. He bought the Coates Estate, part of the open countryside that lay to the north and west of the Nor' Loch.

Another resident was Sir William Dick of Braid, a very wealthy merchant and also Lord Provost of the City. He gave financial support to the Covenanters and then to Charles II after the execution of his father, Charles I in 1649. Sir William was heavily fined by Oliver Cromwell and was reduced to poverty. He travelled to London to plead his case but was imprisoned for debt. He was released but died in his Westminster lodgings in 1655.

An earlier resident of the Close was Adam Bothwell, Bishop of Orkney (1527 - 1593) and the uncle of John Napier of Merchiston, inventor of logarithms. Bishop Adam Bothwell had officiated at the marriage of Mary, Queen of Scots to Francis Hepburn, Earl of Bothwell on 15th May 1567 - just weeks after the murder of Mary's husband Henry Darnley. For this Bishop Boswell was roundly criticised by the General Assembly of the Church of Scotland. However the Assembly and the Protestant lords had to turn to him after Mary's enforced abdication on July 24th 1567 to crown the one - year old King James VI.

This was because Scotland's principal churchman, the Archbishop of St Andrews, refused to carry out the ceremony. Bothwell was again questioned by the Assembly concerning his faith and responsibilities. However he was a survivor. He gave up his bishopric and was appointed a Lord of Session and acted as an adviser to James VI.

Nearby Advocate's Close was first recorded as Cant's Close in 1475 when it was the home of Harry Cant, a wealthy merchant. The Close was extended by his nephew Alexander Cant but he was beaten to death by his wife and mother-in-law in 1535. The Close was then the residence of Clement Cor. His initials and those of his wife, Helen Bellenden, together with a dated motto of 1590 can still be seen. The Close is named after Sir James Stewart (1635-1713), the 1st Lord Advocate of Scotland.

A Royal Mile Close

Warriston's Close is named after Sir Archibald Johnson, Lord Warriston. He was one of the authors of the 1638 National Covenant which challenged the right of Charles I to impose changes on the established Presbyterian Church of Scotland. This act of defiance led directly to the English Civil War which resulted in the execution in London of Charles I in 1649 and the rule of Parliament headed by Oliver Cromwell. Warriston served in Cromwell's government.

On the Restoration of Charles II in 1660, Warriston was condemned to death. Warriston fled to Hamburg and from there sought refuge in Rouen. However he was arrested by the French and returned to Scotland. He was tried for treason and sentenced to death. Warriston was executed at the Mercat Cross on 22nd July 1663 just across the High Street from his home.

Lord Warriston

This is a view of the top of the High Street dating from about the 1790s. Ahead is the familiar crown spire of St Giles Kirk dating from the early 1500s. To the left you can see the sign for an inn and the striped pole and basin of a surgeon-barber. In the foreground is a street trader with behind a group of Town Guardsmen in their uniforms.

To the right is one of the public wells with beside it a water caddie with his leather jerkin and barrel slung over his shoulders. His job was to carry water to people's homes. This would sometime involve climbing as many as fourteen flights of stairs in the tall tenements of the Old Town. The large building in front of St Giles Kirk is the Tollbooth – the famous *'Heart of Midlothian.'* There are now brass setts on the ground which mark out the site of the Tollbooth.

The Tollbooth – 'The Heart of Midlothian'

For over 600 years this grim building served as a meeting place for the Scottish Parliament, the law courts and as a notorious prison. The Tollbooth was visited by many Scottish monarchs including Mary, Queen of Scots; held many famous prisoners and was the scene of many executions. One of the most remarkable prisoners held here was Margaret Dickson. She had been sentenced to death in 1742 for the death of her new-born baby. On 2nd September she was taken from the condemned cell, marched up the Lawnmarket and down the West Bow to the Grassmarket where, in front of a huge crowd, she was hanged.

The 'Heart of Midlothian' – the site of the Tollbooth

An Execution in the Grassmarket

She was pronounced dead and, after a fight with some medical students who wanted her body for dissection, her body was cut down and her family put her in a coffin and drove off to Musselburgh where she was to be buried. It was a hot day so they stopped off at Duddingston, then a village outside Edinburgh, and went for a drink in the Sheep's Heid Inn – a pub that you can still visit today.

You can imagine their surprise when on their return they heard noises coming from the coffin. They opened it up to discovered that Margaret was still alive! She had been revived by the jolting of the cart. What were they to do? After much discussion they decided to take her back to Edinburgh.

Here in the Tollbooth, members of the Town Council, the Church and the University debated whether or not she should be hanged again. In the end they decided that as she had been already pronounced dead it was an act of God that she had been restored to life. So she was set free and as 'Half-Hangit Maggie' she lived for another forty years.

Perhaps the most infamous incident took place in September 1736 when the commander of the Town Guard, Captain John Porteous, was dragged from the Tollbooth cells and lynched by an angry mob. Porteous had ordered his men to fire on the crowd after the hanging of a popular smuggler Andrew Wilson. Some ten people were killed and many more injured. Although condemned to death, his sentence had been suspended while an appeal by Porteous was considered by the government in London. The Edinburgh mob took the law into their own hands and hanged Porteous from a barber's pole in the Grassmarket. Despite the promise of a large reward, no-one was ever punished for this outrageous crime. The Tollbooth was demolished in 1817.

The Edinburgh Town Guard

St Giles Kirk – before the 1829 Restoration.

A church has stood on this spot for nearly 1000 years. The distinctive crown steeple above you dates from the reign of James IV, killed at the Battle of Flodden in 1513. According to tradition St Giles was an Athenian who lived a hermit's life in France in the 7th century. Traditionally he saved the life of a deer from a hunting party led by the King of the Franks. A deer is still part of Edinburgh's Coat of Arms. It was perhaps as a result of the close trading links with France that St Giles was adopted as the patron saint of Edinburgh.

In the 15th century Sir William Preston gifted what was claimed to be the arm bone of St Giles to the church. The Preston Aisle, which can still be seen inside the St Giles, was built to celebrate this event. Much damage was done to the church's interior at the time of the Reformation in 1559. Stained glass windows were smashed and statues destroyed. A life-size image of St Giles was thrown into the Nor' Loch and the arm bone of the saint disappeared. John Knox the leading Protestant reformer in Scotland became the first minister of the new Presbyterian church.

Since 1560, Scotland had been (and of course still is) a Protestant country. Led by John Knox, minister of St Giles, Scotland adopted a Presbyterian form of Christian worship. The Church of Scotland is a democratic church with a very simple order of service and no head of the church like the Pope or the monarch, who is Head of the Church of England. In 1637 though, King Charles I was determined to force the Church of Scotland to become like the Church of England with the king as the head of the church supported by bishops and archbishops. It was announced that St Giles was now to be a Cathedral. Bishops and an Archbishop were reintroduced. This was too much for the Scots.

A new English prayer book was introduced which provoked a riot. Amongst the congregation was Jenny Geddes, a street seller of herbs, who was sitting on her stool to hear the service. Feelings were running high. When James Hannay, the Dean of Edinburgh started to read from the Prayer Book, she stood up and shouted:

"Dinna ye say mass in my lug! Tak' this for his majesty!"

An enraged Jenny Geddes flung her stool at the Dean narrowly missing his head. There was uproar. The service was abandoned. That stool was to lead to the English Civil War and to the execution of King Charles in January 1649.

The present exterior dates only from 1829 when it was felt that the old stonework was in need of repair. The decision to knock down parts of the old church and to reface the building was hugely unpopular. A visit inside the church is certainly to be recommended. There you will be able to step back in time. For over centuries the kings and queens of Scots have worshipped here. The huge central pillars date from the 12th century.

A more recent addition is the Chapel of the Order of the Knights of the Thistle, Scotland's ancient Order of Chivalry. You will find this at the rear of the church to the right (to the south-east of the altar). The Chapel was designed by the famous Scottish architect Sir Robert Lorimer in 1909.

To the south of St Giles lies Parliament Square. For centuries this was the burial ground for Edinburgh. You might just spot a plaque in the car park beside the number '23' that traditionally marks the grave of John Knox. The buildings around you date from the early 1800s and are part of the Scottish law courts. As you can see they are built in the then popular classical style of architecture that was modelled on the buildings of ancient Greece and Rome.

Parliament Square

Across the courtyard is a doorway, number 11, which leads you into Parliament Hall, home to Scotland's Parliament from 1640 until 1707, when the Three Estates, as Scotland's Parliament was called, voted to join with the English Parliament in an Act of Union. This was hugely unpopular and there were riots in the streets of Edinburgh as the Union was debated here. Just where you are standing, armed soldiers from the Castle struggled to prevent an angry mob from storming the building. The Act of Union was passed by 110 votes to 67. Ordinary Scots, who of course didn't have a vote in those days, were incensed at the loss of what they saw as Scotland's historic independence. Petitions like this from Dunfermline were typical of the public mood:

"We humbly beseech the Honourable Estates (the Scottish Parliament) *and do confidently expect that you will not allow of any such Union; but that you will support and preserve entire the Sovereignty and Independence of this Crown and Kingdom..."*

In all 96 petitions were submitted to the Estates. Not one supported the proposed Act of Union.

Robert Burns came to the Parliament building some 80 years after the event and voiced the feelings of many people angered by the bribes given to leading Scots to support the Union when he wrote:

> *"O, would or I had seen the day*
> *That treason thus could sell us,*
> *My auld grey head had lien in clay*
> *Wi' Bruce and loyal Wallace!*
> *But pith and power, till my last hour,*
> *I'll mak' this declaration:*
> *We're bought and sold for English gold—*
> *Such a parcel of rogues in a nation!"*

Parliament Hall is also well worth a visit. After passing through security you can admire the magnificent original 1630s hammer-beam ceiling made of Scandinavian Oak. This is now part of the Scottish Law Courts so you may see a bewigged Advocate pacing and up and down in close discussion with a client.

Parliament Square in the 1700s

Now make your way past the equestrian statue of King Charles II made of lead which dates from 1685 and is the oldest of its kind in the UK. Ahead of you is a smaller statue erected in 2008. This is of James Braidwood, Edinburgh's first Firemaster, who was in charge of operations during the Great Fire of Edinburgh in November 1824. The stretch of the High Street running from where you are standing down to the Tron Kirk and southwards to the Cowgate was destroyed.

The fire started at 10.00pm on the night of 15th November 1824 in an engraver's workshop on the second floor of a tenement in Old Assembly Close.

The City's Fire Brigade was quickly on the scene but their work was hampered by the height of the tenement buildings. A strong wind blew sparks and burning embers. All that night and the next day the fire spread. At one time it was feared that St Giles and Parliament Hall would be destroyed by the flames. This is how the scene was reported in a local newspaper, the *'Edinburgh Evening Courant'*

"The scene was now awfully grand...The whole horizon was completely enveloped in lurid flame...The County Hall at one time appeared like a palace of light and the venerable steeple of St Giles reared itself amid the bright flames like a spectre awakened to behold the fall and ruin of the devoted City."

James Braidwood

Fortunately the wind eased and a downpour on November 17th eventually put out the fires. The damage was immense with twenty-five tenements totally destroyed and many others damaged. Thirteen people lost their lives including two firemen. The spire of the Tron Kirk collapsed but fortunately the church itself was saved. James Braidwood was widely praised for his efforts. He was appointed as the first Firemaster of London in 1833 and was killed while on duty in 1861 at the Tooley Street Fire near London Bridge.

The Great Fire of November 1824

The Mercat Cross traditionally was the centre of Scottish burgh life. It was here that important local and national announcements were made. People would meet to chat, to exchange news and to conduct their business. There was also a darker side to the Cross as it was here that many executions were carried out. Amongst those executed here were the Marquess of Montrose (1650) and his arch-enemy the Marquess of Argyll (1661). Both men have memorials in nearby St Giles. Lord Warriston was likewise executed here in 1663.

It was also at the Cross that criminals were publicly punished, often with great cruelty. In 1652, two Englishmen made the mistake of drinking a toast to the exiled Charles II. They were arrested. They were given thirty-nine lashes and were then nailed by their ears to the gallows beside the Cross. This Cross was restored in 1885 by William Ewart Gladstone, the local MP and Liberal Prime Minister. The Mercat Cross is where important national proclamations are still made.

The old Mercat Cross of Edinburgh

The site of the original Cross which had stood for centuries, is marked by special stones just ahead of you outside the Festival Fringe Office. This Cross was demolished in 1751 to try to persuade citizens to move their business inside to the planned new Royal Exchange, the imposing building across the street. The Exchange, opened in 1761 was the brainchild of George Drummond, six times the Lord Provost of Edinburgh. Drummond was determined to improve the appearance of the city. The work was designed by Robert Adam and carried out by John Fergus. This is a courtyard development open to the street through a single-storey rusticated screen. The Corinthian pilasters were added by John Fergus. It became the City Chambers in 1811 and is still the Headquarters of the City of Edinburgh Council. Beneath the City Chambers is Mary King's Close partially abandoned in the 1640s after an outbreak of the plague.

The Mercat Cross and the City Chambers

The statue beside the Mercat Cross is of Adam Smith, the well-known economist and author of *'The Wealth of Nations'* published in 1776. Edinburgh at that time was the home of several men of learning including Adam Smith, David Hume the philosopher and historian, Professor Joseph Black the chemist, James Hutton the geologist and Professor Alexander Munro who over a career spanning fifty years trained some 10000 medical students the skills of anatomy. This was truly was a *'Golden Age'* for Edinburgh and the City was nicknamed *'The Athens of the North'*. One contemporary remarked that:

"There is not a city in Europe that enjoys such a singular and noble privilege...Here I stand at what is called the Cross of Edinburgh and can in a few minutes take 50 men of genius and learning by the hand."

The Statue of Adam Smith

Much of this was due to the reputation of the University of Edinburgh which attracted academics and students from many countries. When the foundation stone of what is known today as *'The Old Quad'* was laid in 1789, the University had over 1000 students of whom some 400 were medical students.

Across the High Street is Anchor Close. This Close dates back to 1521 and is named after the Anchor Tavern which was another popular Edinburgh *'howff'* (pub). The Close was the home of Provost George Drummond (1687-1766). He did more than any other citizen of his day to bring improvements to the Old Town and to promote the construction of the New Town. The Close also held the premises of William Smellie the well-known Edinburgh printer who, with the engraver Andrew Bell, produced the first edition of the *'Encyclopedia Britannica'* in 1768 and the Edinburgh Edition of the Poems of Robert Burns in 1787.

Just further down this north side of the High Street is North Foulis Close, the 16th century home of the the Foulis family, the hereditary Lords of Colinton. The plaque commemorates James Gillespie of Spylaw, who along with his brother John, had a well-known tobacconist and snuff shop here. The brothers were typically canny Scots' businessmen who gradually amassed a small fortune from their business. In 1759 they purchased the snuff mills in Colinton. James oversaw the manufacturing side of the business while John managed the shop. The brothers never married and lived very frugally. The one luxury that they allowed themselves was the purchase of a bright yellow coach. This prompted Henry Erskine, the witty Lord Advocate to remark:

*"Wha wad hae thocht it
That noses could hae bocht it!"*

Shrewd investments in tobacco in the new United States further increased their wealth. John died in 1795 followed by James in 1797. He divided his fortune between two charitable enterprises – a hospital for needy senior citizens and a school for poor children, now of course James Gillespie's High School.

James and John Gillespie

There are two plaques above the Close entrance. John Kay (1742 – 1826) lived here. He was born in Dalkeith, moved to Edinburgh and set up a successful barbershop in Parliament Square. He was an excellent self-taught caricaturist and engraver. Kay began sketching his customers. He displayed these sketches in his shop window. They proved very popular. He retired from hairdressing and became a full-time caricaturist. In all he sketched some 900 'portraits' of his contemporaries. Some 350 of these were collected and published in 1837 by his friend Hugh Paton.

A self- portrait of John Kay

The other plaque commemorates Dr Elsie Inglis (1864-1917). She was one of the first women to qualify as a doctor and worked helping the poor in the Old Town. She was also a leading Scottish suffragette campaigning for the rights of women. In the First World War, she led a Scottish Hospital Unit in the Balkans and was captured by the Austrians when she refused to abandon her patients.

Released, she continued to work in appalling conditions. By now she was very ill. She was shipped home. Too weak to make the journey back to Edinburgh, she died in Newcastle on 26th November 1917. Her body was brought back to Edinburgh and, after a packed service at St Giles, she was buried with full military honours in the Dean Cemetery.

Just down from North Foulis Close is Fleshmarket Close. This led to the 18th century Fleshmarket which was located on the banks of the Nor' Loch. It was an early home of the famous Henry Dundas, Viscount Melville (1742-1811), the *'uncrowned King of Scotland'* at the end of the 18th century. The northern section of the Close was swept away when Cockburn Street was constructed in 1859. This linked the High Street with the new Waverley Station.

Cross over to the south side of the High Street towards the New Assembly Close. Notice the brass setts in the road. These mark the site of the City Guardhouse which once stood here. It was demolished in 1785.

The Old City Guardhouse

The Entrance to New Assembly Close

The first attempts at introducing Dancing Assemblies were fiercely opposed by the Church of Scotland. The Church strongly disapproved of the fashionable young men and women of Edinburgh enjoying themselves. However in 1720 an Assembly was successfully opened in Old Assembly Close just further up the High Street. The behaviour of the young dancers was though strictly controlled. For many years this was the task of Miss Nicky Walker, a sister of the Earl of Mansfield. She sat on a high chair and kept strict order. One contemporary described the scene:

"These Assemblies began about five and stopped at eleven. When the bells of St Giles rung out the hour. Miss Nicky waved her fan, the fiddlers stopped playing and the dancing was at an end."

The Assembly moved here to New Assembly Close in 1776. The behaviour though of the dancers had slipped due in part to the introduction of the popular Scottish Country Dancing.

Writing in 1783, an Edinburgh lawyer, Hugo Arnot noted that:

"Minuets are given up and country dances only are used, which often have a resemblance to a game of romps than elegant and graceful dancing. Dress, particularly by the men, is much neglected; and many of them reel from the tavern flustered with wine, to an Assembly of as elegant and beautiful women as any in Europe"

The Tron Kirk in the 1700s

Further down on the south side of the High Street stands the Tron Kirk. The name *'Tron'* comes from the old Scots' word for a weighing beam and here in the Middle Ages goods were weighed and checked by City officials before being released for sale. The Tron Kirk was built in the 1630s to house some of the overflowing congregation from St Giles. If you look closely at the spire you will see that today's spire is different from the one that you can see in this picture.

This is because the original spire was burnt down in the Great Fire of 1824. The Tron Kirk closed for worship in 1952. The area of the High Street around the Tron Kirk was for many years the gathering place for Edinburgh folk celebrating Hogmanay. The bells of the church rang in the New Year. Now *'Edinburgh's Hogmany'* culminates with the celebrations in Princes Street a wonderful fireworks display set against the background of Edinburgh Castle.

You will also notice that the area on either side of the kirk has changed as well. In the 1780s the area was cleared and Blair Street and Hunter Square were built. They are named after Lord Provost James Hunter Blair who led the successful campaign to open up a new route to the spreading suburbs to the south. This was of course the South Bridge. Hunter Blair also championed the construction of new premises for *'the toun's college'* – the *'Old Quad'* of the University of Edinburgh – started in 1789.

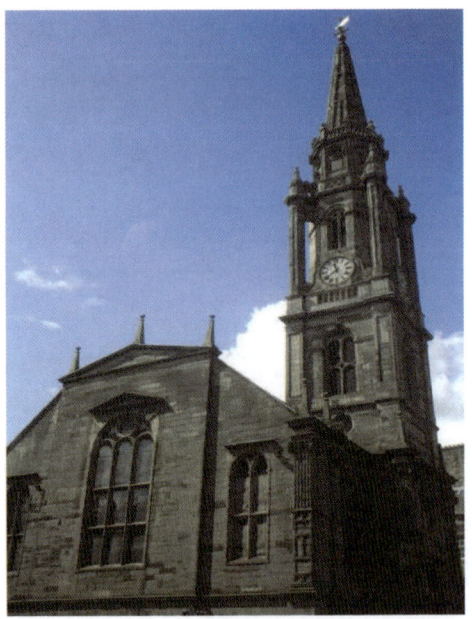

The Tron Kirk

Now move to the traffic light crossing at the junction of the South Bridge and the North Bridge. Although the two bridges are aligned, they were in fact built some twenty years apart. The foundation stone for the North Bridge was laid in October 1765. The bridge was to be the vital link between the Old Town and the planned New Town to the north. When the South Bridge was built in the 1780s part of the Tron Kirk had to be demolished so that the two bridges could be aligned.

Laying the Foundation Stone for the University of Edinburgh's new building, known as the 'Old Quad', 1789

Just down from the traffic lights is Niddry Street formally known as Niddry's Wynd. In 1732, this was the scene of a shocking abduction. Lady Grange, the estranged wife of Lord Grange, brother of the powerful Earl of Mar, had taken exception to her husband's affairs.

Niddry Street

Lady Grange was the daughter of John Chiesley of Dalry, the man hanged at the Mercat Cross for killing Lord President Lockhart in March 1689. She too seems to have had something of a temper. Lady Grange took up lodgings here in the Wynd to keep an eye on her husband. Lord Grange objected to this and arranged to have his wife abducted. So on the night of 22nd January 1732, Lady Grange was seized on her way home by a gang of Highlanders. In the struggle to break free poor Lady Grange had some of her teeth knocked out. She was bundled on to a horse, wrapped in a tartan blanket and taken from Edinburgh.

For several years her friends were at a loss to know what had happened to her. Then word reached them through a smuggled message that she had been taken to the remote island of St. Kilda off the north-west coast of Scotland. At once her friends organised a rescue mission and chartered a ship to save her. Sadly word of this reached her captors and she was taken away again, this time to the Isle of Skye. There poor Lady Grange went mad and died in 1749.

Her death was noted by her estranged husband Lord Grange:

"I most heartily thank you my dear friend for the timely notice of the death of that person. It would be a ridiculous untruth to pretend grief for it; but as it brings to my mind a train of various things for many years back it gives me concern....I long for the particulars of her death which you are pleased to tell me I am to have by the next post."

Because of his political influence, the heartless Lord Grange was never punished for his crime.

At the foot of Niddry Street is St Cecilia's Hall. This was built in 1762 by the architect Robert Mylne for the Edinburgh Music Society. The building was modelled on the Opera House in Parma. The concert hall could seat 500. The last concert was performed here in 1793. The building has had an interesting history since then. It has been a Baptist Church, A Freemasons' Hall, a school and for a while after 1945, it served as a dance hall. The building was very tastefully restored in 1960 and is part of the University of Edinburgh's School of Music. Performances can once again be enjoyed in the beautiful concert hall.

St Cecila's Hall

The next street down from Niddry Street is Blackfriars' Street This was the scene of a violent street brawl in 1520 when supporters of the powerful Douglas and Hamilton families fought for control of the young King James V. Street brawls known as *'Tulzies'* were all too common in the Old Town of Edinburgh. This one though was the worst. This bloody affray, known as *'Cleanse the Causeway'*, left over eighty Hamiltons dead and dying in the street.

About 50 metres down on your right is a building, now a hostel, but formally the town house of the Earl of Morton, one of the key players in the downfall of Mary, Queen of Scots. Morton was one of the conspirators whose men murdered Henry Darnley, husband of the Queen in 1567. He was strangled in a garden about 400 metres down from here. Mary made the fatal mistake of marrying Francis Hepburn, the Earl of Bothwell just a few weeks after this. Bothwell was also guilty of the murder of Darnley. This caused outrage. Bothwell fled Scotland while Mary was forced to abdicate. She then escaped to England where she was executed in 1587. Morton too was executed at the Mercat Cross in 1581 for his part in Darnley's murder.

The Earl of Morton's 'Palace'

Move back to the High Street and cross over to Paisley Close.

Paisley Close

By the middle of the 19th century many of the Old Town tenements had become grossly overcrowded as poorer people flocked in from the countryside and from Ireland desperately looking for work. The population of the city trebled in just 100 years to reach 222000 in 1861. With no appropriate local authority regulations, conditions deteriorated dramatically. What had once been good homes were reduced to miserable, overcrowded slums. With no proper sanitation, conditions were appalling. The dreaded cholera was a regular visitor causing the deaths of hundreds. A local doctor, Alex Wood recorded that:

"In the Middle Meal Market Stairs are 59 rooms…In these dwell 248 individuals divided into 56 families…There is no water, no water closet, no sink…It is not difficult to imagine the state of wet and filth in which they must continually be."

It was not widely accepted in those days that it was the job of the government to interfere to improve ordinary peoples' lives. This comfortable view though was to be rudely shattered when tragedy struck here in Paisley Close.

"One of the most appalling disasters…occurred yesterday morning. An immense, tall and thickly populated tenement…suddenly gave way…floor carrying down floor and in a few moments buried the unwarned inmates in the ruins."
(Edinburgh Evening Courant 25th November 1861.)

In all 35 people were killed and many more injured. Rescuers frantically searched the rubble for any survivors. Suddenly a faint voice was heard crying from underneath the rubble.
"Heave awa' lads, I'm no deid yet."

This was a young survivor of the disaster, Joseph McIvor, who was pulled safely from the ruins and duly entered Edinburgh's folk lore with his *"Heave awa"*. (Note though the anglicised version above the Close entrance. It was carved by an English sculptor).

Shocked by this tragedy, the City persuaded Parliament to pass the Edinburgh Old Town Improvement Act in 1867. Lord Provost William Chambers pushed through a wide-ranging programme of improvements. Old houses were demolished, streets widened and, most importantly, clean water was provided. Edinburgh's first Medical Officer for Health, Dr. Henry Littlejohn, was appointed. Over the next 30 years, nearly 90% of the Old Town was demolished in the name of progress. While today we may regret this loss of Edinburgh's historic heritage, drastic action was needed to improve the quality of life for the thousands of people crammed into the overcrowded, unhealthy Old Town.

Across the street is the City's famous Museum of Childhood.

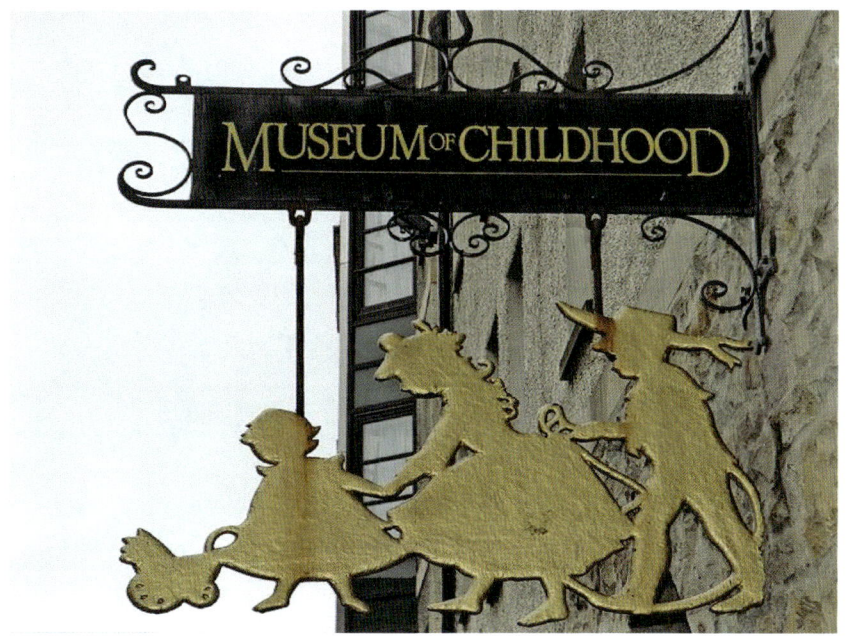

The Entrance Sign of the Museum of Childhood

The Museum of Childhood, run by the City of Edinburgh Council, is a collection of toys from around the world. The Museum moved to this 18th century tenement in 1957.

The collection was gifted to the City by Patrick Murray, an Edinburgh Councillor, who had a passion for collecting toys and childhood memorabilia, the Museum was the first in the world to be dedicated to children's toys. The Museum attract some 25000 visitors annually and entrance is free.

Move further down the High Street to John Knox's House. You are now standing beside one of the old public wells that brought water down from the town reservoir situated at the top of Castlehill.

John Knox's House

The Well stands in front of two of Edinburgh's oldest surviving houses – the rubble-built Moubray House with its traditional outside stone stair and, ahead of you, the better-known John Knox's House with its decorated frontage and timbered gallery. Both of these houses date from the early 1500s but are built on much older foundations. In 1544 an English army captured Edinburgh and set the town on fire. Henry VIII was trying to force the Scots to agree to the marriage of the infant Mary, Queen of Scots to Henry's young son, Prince Edward. The Scots refused so an enraged Henry issued this brutal order.

"Put all to fire and sword; burn Edinburgh town; beat down and overthrow the Castle; sack Holyrood House, putting man, woman and child to fire and sword without any exception where any resistance shall be made against you"

Under the Earl of Hertford's command, an English army landed near Leith and advanced on Edinburgh. The Lord Provost, Sir Adam Otterburn, was ordered to surrender the burgh. He refused. So the English army attacked and smashed their way through the Netherbow Port, one of the principal gates into the burgh that stood just in front of you below John Knox's House. The Edinburgh citizens fought bravely to defend their homes but were overwhelmed. Hundreds were killed. When night fell all resistance had been crushed. Only the Castle held out against the invaders. An English officer described of what happened next:

"It was determined utterly to ruinate and destroy the said town with fire…so that within the walls nor in the suburbs was left any house unburnt besides the innumerable booties, spoils, and pillages that our soldiers brought from thence…Also we burnt the Abbey and the Palace"

As well as setting fire to Edinburgh, the retreating English army set about destroying the Border towns and abbeys that lay in its path. No wonder then that Scots refer to this grim time as *'The Rough Wooing'*. The English repeated the punishment in 1545 and again in 1547 but still the stubborn Scots refused to give in to Henry's demands. In 1548 Mary was sent to France for her own safety. She remained there until 1561. So a new, stone-built Edinburgh, including these two houses, arose from the ashes.

However it is very doubtful if this was ever the home of John Knox – though he may have spent a short time here near the end of his life in 1572. Interestingly, while Knox has the reputation of being a narrow-minded killjoy, he married his second wife Margaret Stewart in 1564 when he was 54 and she was only 16. She bore him 3 daughters.

So if it was not John Knox's house, then who stayed here? During the reign of Mary, Queen of Scots, it was the home of James Mossman, a goldsmith, and his wife Margaret Arras whose arms and initials can be seen on the wall along from the figure of Moses pointing to God represented by the sun.

The Coat of Arms of James Mossman and Margaret Arras

The house also carries a religious motto, a popular practice of those days. Mossman's father refashioned the Scottish Crown for James V, father of Mary, Queen of Scots. James Mossman was executed in 1573 for his loyalty to Mary.

Even if this was not the home of John Knox, the tradition that it was, saved the house from demolition when so much of the historic Old Town was being swept away. Now with its hand-painted ceiling and surviving wooden gallery, it is preserved as an interesting example of a 16th century town house. Linked to John Knox's House is the Scottish Storytelling Centre complete with performance space, café and a bookshop located at street level in the original 'luckenbooth' (or shop) of John Knox's House.

Make your way across the High Street into Tweeddale Court. Some of the property that surrounds you dates back to the early 1500s. Stop beside the small building on your right. This is thought to be a shed for sedan chairs used for carrying well-off folk around 18th century Edinburgh. The old wall beside you is believed to be the only surviving section of the King's Wall built during the reign of James II in the 15th century to protect the town from the English.

Section of the 15th century King's Wall

The house at the foot of the Court belonged to the Marquesses of Tweeddale. It was improved by Robert Adam in the 1750s. In 1791 it was taken over by the British Linen Bank. A famous unsolved murder took place here just where you are standing. On a dark November evening in 1806 a child stumbled across the body of Thomas Begbie, a bank messenger. He had been stabbed to death and robbed of £4000. Although most of the money was later found hidden in a wall, no-one was ever brought to trial. However it was widely believed that the murderer was a well-known criminal James Mackoull who died in prison in 1820 while awaiting trial for another murder.

Tweedale Court Mansion

Now move out of the Court back to the High Street. Ahead of you on the facing wall you can see a carved plaque showing the Netherbow Port. This was the ancient fortified gateway into Edinburgh that was eventually pulled down in 1764. You can see the outline of the Netherbow Port marked in brass plates in the road beside the traffic lights.

The Netherbow Port

The final close of the High Street is appropriately named 'The World's End' because for Edinburgh folk this was the end of their world in olden times.

The World's End Close Entrance

5. THE CANONGATE

The Canongate Tollbooth

MAP 4

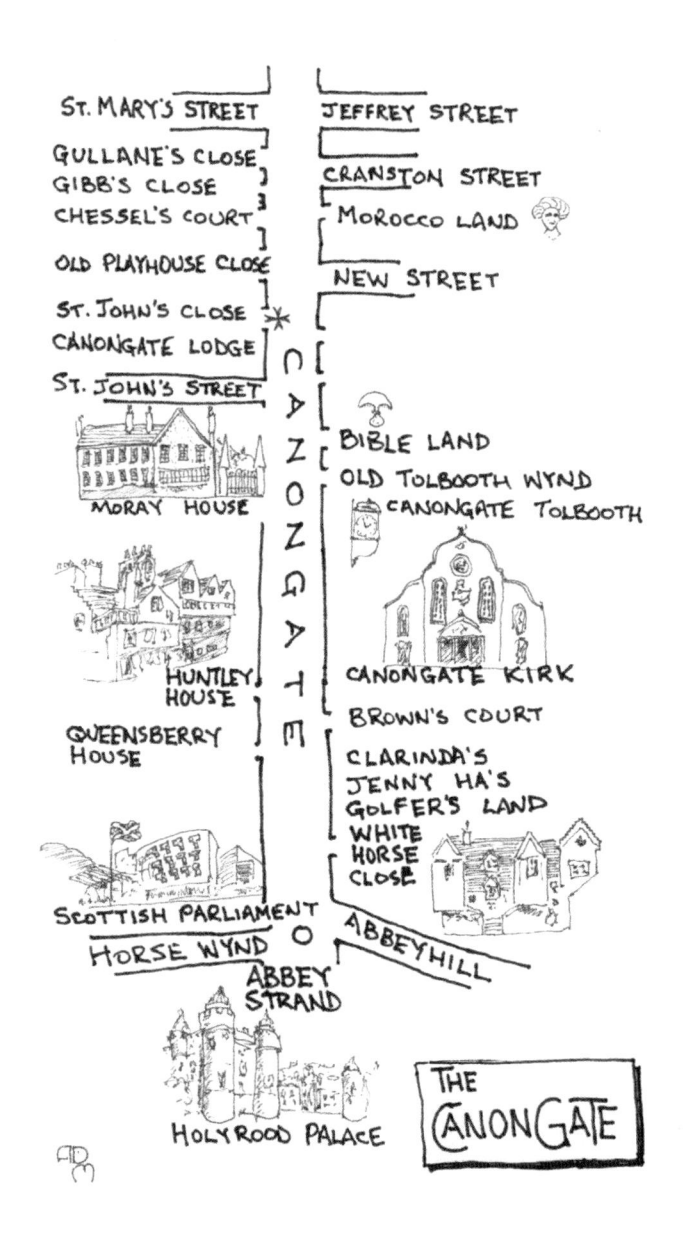

Before you set off down the Canongate, look at the building ahead of you across St Mary's Street. You should see the outline of a stag's head. This is the emblem of the separate burgh of the Canongate founded by King David I in 1128. The Canongate remained a separate burgh until 1856 when it was merged with Edinburgh. *'Canongate'* means the way of the canons or monks, (*'gate'* is an old Scots word for a street). The monks came originally from Holyrood Abbey, the ruins of which stand ahead of you at the foot of the Royal Mile.

The Emblem of the Canongate on Canongate Kirk

The founding of the Abbey is one of the best-known of Edinburgh legends. Ignoring advice from his courtiers, David I chose to go hunting on a saint's day in 1128. With a few companions he rode into the great forest of Drumsheugh which lay in the shadow of Arthur's Seat. Suddenly an enormous stag leapt out in front of the king and he fell from his horse. The stag was just about to gore David when a cross appeared in the king's hand and the stag disappeared into the trees. David promised to found an abbey at the spot of his miraculous escape and so Holyrood Abbey was built.

Cross over St Mary's Street and enter the Canongate. Like every Close and Wynd of the Royal Mile, St Mary's Street has a story to tell. Originally known as St Mary's Wynd, it led to St Mary's Chapel. In 1530 a local resident, Marion Clark, was taken outside Edinburgh and drowned for concealing the plague and attending mass at the chapel.

Entrance to Gibb's Close

Just a few metres down on the right-hand side of the Canongate you will pass Gullan's Close. Just beyond this is an entrance marked Gibb's Close. This was the scene of one of the worst murders carried out by the villainous Burke and Hare. So who were these criminals?
The clue lies in an old Edinburgh children's rhyme:

> *Up the Close and doon the stair.*
> *But and ben wi' Burke and Hare,*
> *Burke's the butcher,*
> *Hare's the thief.*
> *Knox the man who buys the beef!"*

By the end of the 1700s, Edinburgh had one of the largest medical schools in the world. So there was a huge demand for bodies for dissection to teach anatomy to the students. There was though a problem. These were the days without proper means to preserve corpses and the University's medical school was only allowed the body of one executed a criminal a year plus any unclaimed bodies that were found in the streets. This was nowhere near enough for the medical school. So there arose the practice of *'grave-robbing'* whereby freshly buried corpses were dug up at dead of night by criminals known as *'resurrectionists'* who then sold the bodies to the doctors with no questions asked.

William Burke

Now it's often claimed that Burke and Hare were grave-robbers. But they weren't. They didn't bother taking the risk of sneaking into graveyards at night and risking arrest. They just murdered people instead.

William Burke and William Hare were both Irish labourers who had come to Scotland to look for work.

They ended up in a dingy lodging house in Tanners Close at the west end of the Grassmarket. When an old lodger called Mr Donald died owing £4 in rent, the enterprising pair packed the body in a case and wheeled it through the Grassmarket and headed off to nearby Surgeon Square.

Dr. Robert Knox

There they sold it to one of the leading medical lecturers of the day, Dr Robert Knox, a former army doctor who had served at the Battle of Waterloo. Burke and Hare got nearly £8 for the body. A good week's wage for a working man in those days was only about £1. The temptation to make some easy money, without much in the way of hard work, proved too much for them.

It will never be known exactly how many people they killed. But between Christmas 1827 and October 1828 at least 16 were murdered by the villainous pair. Their victims tended to be down and outs who were lured to the lodging house, plied with cheap whisky and then suffocated.

The larger man Burke would sit on the victim's chest, while Hare would hold their mouth and nostrils tightly shut. This method of killing of course left no obvious signs of violence so, again no questions were asked by Dr Knox and his staff and the Irishmen as much as £12 a body the richer. One of their victims was Mary Paterson, a local prostitute. She was lured to Gibb's Close, murdered in the usual way, packed in a tea chest and carted off to Dr Knox. He was so struck by her beauty that he sent for a local artist, Mr. Oliphant, and had the poor girl painted in the nude as though she was sleeping.

The body of Mary Paterson

Again though, there were no questions asked. The murderers were only found out when a young couple came to the lodging house looking for an old relative, Mrs Docherty. Instead they found her body, all packed up and ready to be taken to Surgeons' Square. Burke and Hare were arrested. Hare though was never brought to justice. He turned King's Evidence. So it was only Burke and his partner Helen McDougal who were charged.

The trial started on Christmas Eve, 1828. Burke was found guilty but the case against Helen McDougal was found *'Not Proven'* and she was released. Burke was sentenced to death. The trial judge Lord Boyle, was so horrified with the details of the murders that he ordered that Burke be publicly dissected after his execution.

The sentence was carried out on 27th January 1829. Burke was hanged in front of a howling mob. Thousands then followed the corpse to Surgeon's Hall where Burke's body was put on display. The corpse was then dissected in front of a packed crowd. Parts of his skin were tanned and sold as souvenirs. Burke's skeleton can still be seen in the Museum at Surgeon's Hall. And what of Knox and Hare? Hare fled Edinburgh and died in poverty in London. Knox though continued to practice but his house was attacked and he was forced to leave the city. He settled in London and wrote books about fishing. He continued to lecture for many years, dying in 1862.

The Death Mask of William Burke

Morocco Land

Look across the Canongate for the little statue of a Moor set above the street level. This marks the site of an old tenement known as Morocco Land. Edinburgh tradition tells of the arrival of a fleet of Moorish pirates in the year 1645. Edinburgh was stricken by plague and too weak to defend itself. All seemed lost. However (so the story goes!), the Moorish captain turned out to be an Edinburgh man, Andrew Gray. As a youth, he had been sentenced to death for rioting but had escaped from the Tollbooth and fled the burgh, reaching Morocco and becoming a corsair captain. He fell in love with the Lord Provost's daughter; they married and settled in what came to be known as Morocco Land.

About 40 paces further on you will pass Chessel's Court, an attractive development built in 1748 by Archibald Chessel. This was the scene of the infamous Deacon Brodie's botched attempt in 1788 to rob the Excise Office located here. His three accomplices were arrested but Brodie fled to London and from there to Amsterdam but was caught on the eve of his departure to New York. He was brought back and with his fellow-robber George Smith, was hanged at the Tollbooth in October 1788 before a crowd of thousands of spectators.

Chessel's Court

A short distance further down the south side of the Canongate is Old Playhouse Close. This was the home of Edinburgh's first regular theatre. In 1736 a theatre, opened by the poet Alan Ramsay in Carruber's Close in the High Street, was shut down by the Council under pressure from the Edinburgh Presbytery of the Church of Scotland, who strongly disapproved of the theatre and threatened theatre-goers with punishment. This quote gives you a flavour of their feelings

"A company of stage-players who are acting Plays within the precincts of the town have begun with acting one which is filled with horrid swearing, obscenity and expressions of double meaning". (Edinburgh Presbytery 1727.)

Undeterred Edinburgh theatre-lovers tried again and in 1746 opened a theatre here. The new Playhouse was managed by a London actor, Mr John Ryan. Performances were marred by frequent riots.

In 1749, a group of English officers from the Castle loudly demanded that the orchestra play *'Culloden.'* The orchestra instead, to cheers from the crowd, played *'You're welcome Charlie Stewart.'* Incensed, the officers drew their swords and attacked the orchestra.

Other members of the audience rushed to protect the musicians including some Highland Sedan chairmen who hit the officers with their long poles and drove them from the theatre. Shortly after there was a pitched battle in the theatre between two rival groups each claiming ownership of the premises. Much damage was done and the theatre was set on fire.

The Entrance to Old Playhouse Close

On December 14th 1756, the first performance of *'Douglas'* was staged. This was a Scottish tragedy written by John Hume, an ordained minister. This infuriated the Church already hostile to stage performances.

The Edinburgh Presbytery suspended those ministers who attended and warning notices were read out from each pulpit. The Reverend Alexander Carlyle of Inveresk was tried by the East Lothian Presbytery for having attended a performance but the case was dismissed thanks to the intervention of some powerful friends. On the first night, which was a sell-out, some English officers attended. This prompted one theatre-goer to shout out *"Whaur's your Willie Shakespeare now?"*

Hume resigned his position as a minister of the Church of Scotland and moved to London. There he wrote several more plays but none was a successful as *'Douglas'*. Hume returned to Edinburgh and died here in 1808. He served as secretary to Lord Bute and also was a tutor to the prince of Wales. The Canongate theatre was closed in 1769 when the Theatre Royal was opened in the New Town.

The Cross of the Order of the Knights of St John

This emblem in the street marks out an area of the Royal Mile that once was gifted to the Knights of the Order of St. John. This is an old religious military order that had been formed originally during the time of the Crusades to free the Holy Land. At one time this site marked the eastern boundary of the old medieval Edinburgh.

Just a short distance further down you come to the entrance to St John's Street. This street was built in 1768 and proved a popular residence for better-off Edinburgh citizens away from the smells and over-crowding of the Old Town.

Amongst the residents was James Burnett, Lord Monboddo. He was an eccentric judge who lived here until his death in 1799. His home was renowned for the 'learned suppers' he organised at which the table was strewn with roses. Amongst his guests were David Hume and James Hutton. He was interested in the origins of language and published his *'Origins and Progress of Language'* in 1773.

Monboddo was a pioneer evolutionist who was convinced that man was indeed descended from the apes and that there was a midwives' conspiracy. He believed that they cut off the tails of newly-born babies. His beautiful daughter, Elizabeth, enchanted Robert Burns but died tragically of consumption at the age of 25 at Braid Farm. Burns wrote an elegy to her memory.

Lord Monboddo (right) arguing with Hugo Arnot

The one surviving house in St John's Street belongs to the Order of St John. Beside it is the Masonic Lodge Room of the Canongate Lodge, Kilwinning. This was built in 1736 and is the oldest Lodge Room in the world. It was here on
1st February 1787 that Robert Burns was admitted to the Lodge and honoured as *'Caledonia's Bard'*.

The Canongate Kilwinning Masonic Lodge Room

The older turreted house on the corner of St John's Street was where the author Tobias Smollet stayed with his sister during the winter of 1770 – 1771. It was here that he wrote his novel *'The Expedition of Humphrey Clinker'* – a best-seller in its day.

St John's Street

Ahead of you is the impressive balcony and pyramid-capped entrance to Moray House, a fine surviving example of a 17th century townhouse. The property was built originally in 1628 for the Countess of Home and then passed to her daughter, the Countess of Moray in 1645. It is now the Moray House School of Education, part of the University of Edinburgh.

Moray House

Oliver Cromwell stayed here in 1648 and again in September 1650 after his victory over the Scots at the Battle of Dunbar. The first floor room facing onto the balcony has a beautifully decorated original 17th century plaster ceiling. This is where Cromwell set up his headquarters during his occupation of Edinburgh.

In May 1650 a wedding party was being held in this room. This was the celebration of the marriage of the Marquess of Lorne, son of the powerful Marquess of Argyll to Lady Mary Stewart, eldest daughter of the Earl of Moray.

The guests were interrupted by a noise from the street outside. They crowded to the windows and onto the balcony to see below them a cart guarded by soldiers and on that cart was the chained figure of the Marquess of Montrose. A great champion of the executed King Charles I, Montrose had been captured and brought into Edinburgh to face trial. Traditionally the wedding guests shouted abuse at the fallen hero while it is said that the Countess of Argyll spat on him. Montrose was executed as a traitor on the gallows next to the Mercat Cross. Ironically both Argyll and his son were later to suffer a similar fate after the Restoration of Charles II in 1660.

Tucked away amongst the modern buildings of Moray House, is the little garden summer house where traditionally it is said that the terms of the Treaty of Union between Scotland and England were agreed in 1707. At that time, the Lord High Chancellor, the Earl of Seafield, was staying in the house. The Treaty was so unpopular with the Edinburgh mob that this had to be done secretly at dead of night.

The Moray House Garden Summer House

Bible Land

Across the street is Bible Land. The property was built in 1677 by the Incorporation of Cordiners or Shoemakers. If you look above the inscription, taken from Psalm 133, you will see a carving of a shoemaker's rounding knife.

The Canongate Tollbooth is a reminder that for centuries the Canongate was a separate burgh. This was the council headquarters from where the business of the Canongate was carried out. The present building dates from 1591 replacing an older building that stood on this site. The building was refurbished at the end of the 19th century and a clock added. Until 1834 this was used as a debtors' prison. If you look closely you can see the Canongate's coat of arms – the stag's head and a cross.

By the middle of the 1800s, there was serious overcrowding in the Old Town of Edinburgh. By 1865, the area around the Tron Kirk further up the High Street was reckoned to have the densest overcrowding of any European city You can get an impression of just how many people were staying in the Canongate at the start of the last century by looking at the First World War Memorial that is on the wall of the Tollbooth.

The Canongate Tollbooth

The Canongate Tollbooth is the third of the City of Edinburgh museums that can be found on the Royal Mile.

Across the road from you is another surviving house of the 16th century. In fact this is a group of three houses built in 1517 and then extended and linked together in 1570. The houses were originally entered from the adjoining Bakehouse Close that could be closed and defended when trouble threatened. Huntly House was known for years as *'The Speaking House'*. It got its name from the panels put in place in 1570 by the property developer. They are in Latin and seem to suggest that the householder had a quarrel with some of his neighbours! One panel translates as:

"I am the happy man today; your turn may come tomorrow. Why then should you grumble?"

A further tablet goes on to say:
"As you are master of your tongue, so am I master of my ears"

Perhaps peace was restored with his neighbours as the final panel shows the image of the Christian hope of the Resurrection – grains of wheat springing from a handful of bones. Huntly House is also a City of Edinburgh Museum.

Huntly House

Across the road from Huntly House stands the graceful Canongate Kirk. There is a royal pew inside as this is the church used by the Royal Family when they are in residence at Holyrood Palace.

At the entrance stands a statue to the Edinburgh poet Robert Fergusson (1750 – 1774).

Robert Fergusson

Fergusson was born in Edinburgh and educated at the High School and St Andrews University. He took to writing poetry. His output was prolific and he composed 33 poems in Scots and 50 in English. His best work was written in Scots with *'Auld Reekie'* (1773) and *'The Daft Days'* (1772) as the most popular. Here is a verse from *'The Daft Days'*. Fergusson is making fun of the Town Guard

And thou great God o' aquae-vitae! (brandy and whisky)
Wha swayst the empire o' this city
When fou, (drunk) *we're sometimes capernoity,*
(ill-tempered)
Be thou prepared,
Tae save us frae that Black Banditti (thugs)
The City Guard!"

Sadly Fergusson was over-fond of the bottle and so ruined his health. He suffered from deep depression. A fall downstairs reduced him to madness and he died miserably in the town's *'bedlam'* (the lunatic asylum) on the site of present-day Bristo Place.

He was buried in the Canongate Kirkyard in an unmarked pauper's grave. Robert Burns had a great admiration for Fergusson whose work inspired his own. He was so moved by his fate that he paid for a proper headstone and composed a fitting epitaph for Fergusson.

The Canongate Kirk

The striking Canongate Kirk was built in 1688 using money left to the burgh by Thomas Moodie. The kirk was to house the congregation evicted from Holyrood on the orders of King James II. (VII of Scotland) He wanted to use the church at Holyrood to accommodate the Knights of the Thistle, the ancient Scottish Order of Chivalry. The King though never had the opportunity to meet with his Knights at Holyrood as that same year he was forced off the throne because of his Roman Catholicism and fled to France.

The Royal Coat of Arms that you can see above the rose window is that of James's daughter Mary and of her husband William, Prince of Orange who replaced James on the throne in 1688.

The kirkyard is perhaps better-known than the church because of the many famous people buried here. These include Adam Smith, the famous economist, Dugald Stewart the philosopher and Lord Provost George Drummond.

The churchyard is also the last resting place of Mrs. Agnes McLehose with whom Burns fell passionately in love on his first visit to Edinburgh in the winter of 1786 - 1787. The 28 year-old Agnes, known as Nancy, having married at 17 and borne 4 children, had left her husband because of his cruelty. She met Burns at a tea-party. There was an instant attraction between them. They arranged to meet but Burns hurt his leg and was confined to his lodgings. So the pair corresponded with Burns signing his letters as Sylvander and Nancy as Clarinda. Here is taste of their feelings for each other:

> *"I can say with truth, Madam, that I never met a person in my life whom I more anxiously wished to meet again than yourself"*

To which she replied:

> *"I perfectly comprehend....One thing I know, that your words have a powerful effect on me... Pardon any little freedom I take with you."*

The pair did eventually meet but whether or not they became lovers is not known. What is known is that some months later Burns married his pregnant Ayrshire girlfriend Jean Armour. Shortly after, Nancy left for the West Indies.

The news of this prompted Burns to write one of most famous poems which he set to music - *'Ae Fond Kiss'*.

> *"But to see her was to love her*
> *Love but her and love forever*
> *Had we never loved sae kindly*
> *Had we never loved sae blindly*
> *Never met – or never parted*
> *We had ne'er been broken-hearted."*

Nancy lived until 1841. In her journal for 6th December 1831 she recorded:

"This day I can never forget. Parted with Burns in the year 1791, never more to meet in this world. Oh, may we meet in Heaven!"

The Tombstone of 'Clarinda'

Continue down past Clarinda's Coffee House named after the beautiful Mrs. McLehose.

Next is the historic pub Jenny Ha's and just beyond is a plaque recording the site of Golfer's Land, traditionally the home built by John Paterson from the winnings he made partnering the Duke of York (later James II) in a game of golf against two English noblemen played at Leith Links in the 1680s. Scotland prides itself on being the home of golf. Whether the sport actually originated here is a matter of debate. We have though a law of 1457 ordering that:

"the fut ball and the golf be utterly cryit doune and nocht usyt".

With the constant threat of war with England, Scots were to practice archery instead.

Move down just a few paces. Across the road is the imposing Queensberry House, a 17th century mansion once owned by the Marquis of Queensberry, and now part of the complex of buildings that comprise the Scottish Parliament.

By a curious coincidence, it also played a part in the days leading up to the demise of the previous Scottish Parliament which voted to end centuries of independence in 1707. Although Scotland and England had shared the same monarch since 1603, by the end of the 17th century, relations between the two countries had deteriorated. Rather than risk matters getting worse, commissioners were appointed by both countries to see whether terms could be agreed for a Treaty of Union. The Marquis of Queensberry was one of the most important of the Scottish commissioners.

Remember that this was long before the existence of a popular vote. The vast majority of Scots were totally opposed to what they saw as the betrayal of their hard-won independence. Petitions flooded in from all over the country pleading with the Scots' M.Ps. not to agree to the terms. There were riots in many Scottish burghs.

Daniel Defoe, author of *'Robinson Crusoe'* was in Edinburgh acting as an agent for the English government. He sent many alarming reports back to his political masters in London describing this opposition to the proposed Union and the hostility to those seen to support it. Here is part of one of Defoe's reports:

"The rabble…began with Sir Patrick Johnston who was one of the treaters*…First they assaulted his lodgings with stones and sticks then came up the stairs to his door and fell to work to it with great hammers; and had they broke it open… he had without doubt been torn in pieces without mercy."

*One of the commissioners who negotiated the Treaty's terms

Queensberry House

Imagine the scene that night in January 1707. The street around you was filled with an angry mob, furious at what they saw as Queensberry's betrayal of Scotland's independence. Soldiers from the Castle struggled to clear a path for Queensberry's carriage. A roar of anger greeted the sight of the gates opening and the Marquis's coach emerging. Queensberry was surrounded by all of his household who were armed. The House was left deserted apart from a young servant boy and the violently insane James Douglas, the Earl of Drumlanrig, the 10 year old eldest surviving son of Queensberry. Imagine the scene when Queensberry returned from the Parliament to discover his son sitting in front of the kitchen fire turning the spit on which was impaled the body of the unfortunate servant.

Traditionally Queensberry had his son strangled on the spot. However the boy was spirited away to a family estate at Calverley in West Yorkshire. He died there in 1715. and was buried in the local churchyard.

Move down further and on your left you will come to the White Horse Close. For many years this was the home of one of the coaching inns of the Royal Mile. This charming courtyard dates originally from the 16th century. It is thought to have been named after the white horses of Mary, Queen of Scots that were traditionally stabled here. You can almost see the striking figure of the beautiful Queen sweeping past you to inspect her horses. Some two hundred years later, this quiet courtyard would have been filled by Highland officers from the Jacobite army of Bonnie Prince Charlie who were quartered here in September 1745. They clattered past where you are standing on the morning of 30th October on the ill-fated journey that would end in such bloodshed on the battlefield of Culloden in April 1746.

White Horse Close

Move (carefully) across the road and stand in front of the two old buildings that face you. These are surviving houses of the early 1500s known as the Abbey Strand. For centuries these buildings were part of the sanctuary to which debtors could come to escape from their creditors.

The Abbey Strand

Now look at the Parliament building across the street. The new Scottish Parliament came into being by an Act of Parliament in 1998. Following a referendum of the Scottish people held in September 1997, a Parliament returned to Scotland for the first time since 1707. This Parliament was given certain devolved powers such as responsibility for Education and Health. Other matters such as Foreign Policy and Defence remain as the responsibility of the UK Parliament at Westminster.

The first election for the 129 MSPs was held in May 1999 and the Parliament met for the first time in the Assembly Hall at the top of the Mound later that month.

A competition was held for the design of a new Parliament building, This was won by the Spanish architect Enric Miralles. Unfortunately the building programme was fraught with difficulties. There were design problems and delays. To make matters worse the architect died before the building was completed. Costs spiralled and eventually the Parliament came in at a cost of £431m. The building was officially opened by Her Majesty the Queen on 2nd October, 2004.

The Scottish Parliament building remains highly controversial but worth a visit for you to make up your own mind whether this was money well-spent. Nevertheless it is the home of Scotland's Parliament and as such plays a significant part in the life of 21st century Scotland.

The September 2014 referendum on Scottish independence was narrowly defeated in a poll with a huge turnout of 85%. An interesting feature of the referendum was that for the first time in the United Kingdom, the voting age was lowered to 16. Free tours of the Parliament building are available.

The Scottish Parliament Building

Now make your way to the gate and railings to the left of the Holyrood Palace courtyard. Next to the Palace itself you can see the ruins of what was Holyrood Abbey. Holyrood (meaning Holy Cross) Abbey grew to be one of the richest in Scotland. For centuries, kings and queens of Scotland were baptised, married and buried here. The Abbey was severely damaged when an English army sacked Edinburgh in 1544. Although repairs were carried out, the abbey never regained its former grandeur. When the roof collapsed in a storm in 1768, the surviving buildings were abandoned.

Finally we have Holyrood Palace itself started in the early 16th century by James IV but not completed until the 1680s during the reign of King Charles II. The Scottish architect Sir William Bruce matched the original north - west tower with another to the south - west adding new royal apartments built round a central courtyard.

Holyrood is still one of the royal residences. Only the left-hand tower, the north-west tower, had been built when Mary, Queen of Scots, arrived here from France in August 1561.

Holyrood Palace

Her first night at the Palace was far from peaceful! When news spread that Mary was celebrating the detested Catholic Mass in her private chapel, a furious mob tried to storm the Palace.

The Palace's most famous incident took place in that tower on the night of 9th March 1566. A heavily-pregnant Mary was having a quiet supper party with a few close friends and courtiers. Sitting beside her was her secretary, David Rizzio. The close friendship that had developed between Mary and the handsome Italian provoked the anger of her husband Henry Darnley.

Holyrood Palace in the 1600s

Suddenly a group of armed men led by the Earl of Morton and Lord Ruthven burst in looking for Rizzio. Mary herself described what happened next:

"Lord Ruthven and his accomplices advanced on Rizzio who had gone behind my back, and they laid violent hands on him – some struck him over the shoulders and others stood in front of me with pistols, at the door of my room they stabbed him fifty-six times with swords and daggers, at which I was in great fear of my life."

Lord Ruthven, clad in full armour, then berated the shocked Queen for having been too friendly with Rizzio. Mary accused her husband Darnley of being part of the plot to murder Rizzio but he denied it, though his dagger was found planted in Rizzio's chest. Mary never forgave her worthless husband. She retreated to the safety of Edinburgh Castle where in June 1566, she gave birth to the future King James VI. - the first King of the United Kingdom.

Darnley himself was to be murdered shortly after; the Earl of Morton was executed in 1581 for his part in Darnley's killing while Mary, after nineteen years' captivity in England, was executed at Fotheringay Castle in 1587, condemned by her cousin Queen Elizabeth for plotting against her life.

So the Palace is another building that we have passed that is well worth a visit. You can see some of the royal apartments and the room where Rizzio's murder happened. The Palace has an excellent audio guide available for visitors and is a fitting place to end your walk down Edinburgh's historic Royal Mile.

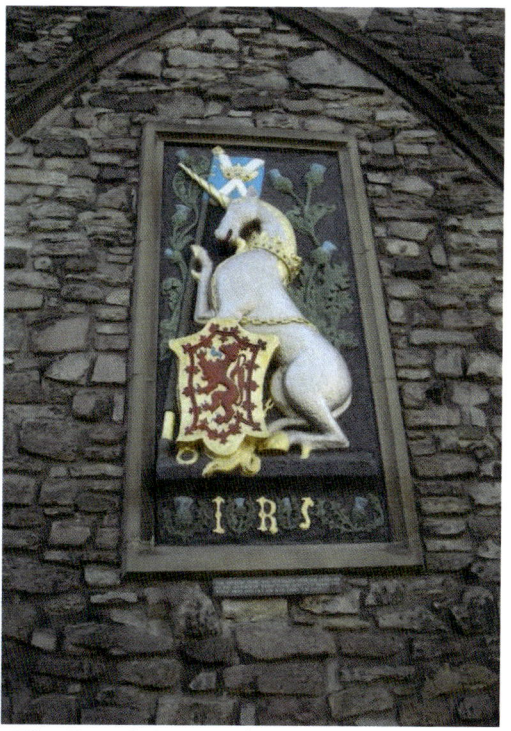

The Royal Arms of James V at Holyrood

INDEX

Abbey Strand 98
Act of Union 45, 87, 95
Adam, Robert 50, 70
Advocate's Close 36, 37
Anchor Close 52
Argyll, Marquess of 49, 86
Arnot, Hugo 57
Arras, Margaret 62
Arthur's Seat 2, 72
'Athens of the North' 51
'Auld Reekie' 28

Bakehouse Close 89
Bannockburn, Battle of 2
Begbie, Thomas 70
Bible Land 88
Black, Professor Joseph 51
Blackfriars' Wynd (Street) 21, 62
Blair, James Hunter 58
Blair Street 58
Bonnie Prince Charlie 9, 13, 97
Boswell, James 27
Bothwell, Adam 36, 37
Boyle, Lord 79
Braidwood, James 47, 48
Brodie's Close 22, 23
Brodie, Deacon William 22, 23, 24, 80
Brownhill, James 27
Brown, John 22
Bruce, Sir William 100
Bryce, George 34
Burke, William 34, 35, 75, 76, 77, 78, 79
Burnett, James, Lord Monboddo 84
Burt, Captain Edmund 28
Burns, Robert 1, 17, 30, 45, 52, 84, 85, 93, 94

Byer's Close 36

Camera Obscura 11
Cannonball House 8, 9, 16
Canongate 4, 5, 72, 73, 79, 88
Canongate Lodge Kilwinning 85
Canongate Kirk 90, 92
Canongate Tollbooth 88, 89
Cant's Close 37
Carlyle, Rev Alexander 83
Carruber's Close 81
Castlehill 4, 6, 8, 10, 13
Chambers, William 64
Charles I 36, 38, 44, 87
Charles II 36, 38, 47, 49, 100
Chessel's Court 23, 80, 81
Chiesley, John 33, 60
City Chambers 50
City Guardhouse 55
City Reservoir 10
Clark, Marion 75
Cleanse the Causeway 62
Cowgate 47
Cromwell, Oliver 36, 38, 86
Culloden, Battle of 9, 13, 97

Darnley, Henry 36, 62, 101, 102, 103
David I 72, 73
Defoe, Daniel 96
Dick, Sir William 36
Dickson, Margaret 40, 41, 42
Dowie's Tavern 33
Drumlanrig, Earl of 97
Drummond, Lord Provost George 50, 52, 93
Dundas, Henry, (Viscount Melville) 55
Dunedin 2

Edinburgh 1, 2, 5,9, 13, 17, 20, 27, 33, 43, 47
Edinburgh Castle 1, 3, 4, 9, 67, 102

Edinburgh's Hogmanay 58
Edinburgh International Festival 4, 16
Edinburgh University 12, 22, 26, 52, 58, 61, 74, 86
Encyclopedia Brittanica 52
Erskine, Henry 53

Fergusson, Robert 90, 91
Fishmarket Close 36
Fleshmarket Close 55
Flodden, Battle of 43

'Gardy – Loo' 28
Geddes, Jenny 44
Geddes, Sir Patrick 12, 13, 22, 26, 30
George IV 33
George IV Bridge 4, 33
Gibb's Close 75, 78
Gillespie, James and John 53
Gladstone, William Ewart 49
Gladstone's Land 25
'Golden Age' 51
Golfer's Land 95
Graham, Gillespie 13
Gray, Andrew 80
Gray, Sir William 28
Grange, Lord and Lady 59, 60, 61
Grassmarket 2, 10, 17, 19, 40, 42, 75
Great Fire 47, 48
Gullan's Close 75
Guthrie, Dr. Thomas 10, 11

Hamilton, Thomas 33
Hannay, James, Dean of Edinburgh 44
Hare, William 75, 76, 77, 78, 79
'Heart of Midlothian' 39, 40
Henry VIII 66
Hepburn, Francis, the Earl of Bothwell 36, 62
Hereford, Earl of 67
High School 21

High Street 4, 21, 28, 31, 34, 35, 38, 39, 52, 53, 56, 71, 88
Holyrood Abbey 5, 73, 92, 100
Holyrood Palace 1, 4, 100, 101, 103
Hub, the 13
Hume, David 27, 51, 84
Hume, Rev John 82, 83
Hunter Square 58
Huntly House 89, 90
Hutton, James 51, 84

Inglis, Dr Elsie 54, 55

Jacobites 9, 97
James II 69
James II (VII) 92, 93
James III 16
James IV 1, 43, 100
James V 62, 103
James VI 3, 21, 37, 102
James Court 12, 27
John Knox's House 4, 66, 67
Johnson, Sir Archibald, Lord Warriston 38, 49
Johnstone Terrace 13

Kay, John 54
Knights of the Thistle 45, 92
Knox, John 4, 66, 67
Knox, Dr Robert 76, 77, 78, 79

Lady Stair's Close 28
Lady Stair's House 12, 29
Lawnmarket 4, 15, 17, 21, 22, 30, 40
Leith Links 95
Liberton's Wynd 33
Littlejohn, Dr Henry 64
Lockhart, Lord President 33
Lorimer, Sir Robert 45

McDougal, Helen 77
Mackoull, James 70
McIvor, Joseph 64
McLehose, Agnes ('Clarinda') 93, 94
McMorran, Baillie James 20, 21, 22

Mary King's Close 50
Mary, Queen of Scots 1, 3, 36, 40, 62, 66, 67, 97, 101, 102, 103
Mercat Cross 33, 38, 49, 50, 51, 60, 62, 87
Miralles, Enric 99
Montrose, Marquess of 49, 87
Moodie, Thomas 92
Moray House 86, 87
Morocco Land 80
Morton, Earl of 62, 102, 103
Mossman, James 68
Moubray House 66
Munro, Professor Alexander 51
Museum of Childhood 65
Milne's Court 26
Mylne, Robert 56

Napier, John 36
Netherbow Port 4, 5, 67, 71
New Assembly Close 55, 56
New Town 59, 83
Niddry Wynd (Street) 59, 61, 62
Nor' Loch 5, 43, 55
North Bridge 59
North Foulis Close 53

Old Assembly Close 47, 56
Old Bank Close 33
Old Playhouse Close 81, 82
Old Town 4, 10, 13, 17, 26, 28, 33, 39, 55, 63, 64, 88
Oliphant, Mr (Artist) 78
Outlook Tower 11, 12

Paisley Close 63, 64

Parliament Hall 45, 47, 48
Parliament Square 45, 54
Paterson, John 95
Paterson, Mary 76
Porteous, Captain John 42
Preston, Sir William 43
Princes Street Gardens 2, 11

Queensberry, Earl of 95, 96, 97
Queensbury House 95, 96, 97

Ramsay, Sir Andrew 19
'Resurrectionists' 76
Riddle's Court 20, 22
Rizzio, David 101, 102, 103
Royal Exchange 50
Royal Mile 1, 2, 4, 5, 10, 12, 17, 20, 23, 24, 35, 36, 73, 97, 103
Robert Bruce, King 1, 2
Rollock, Hercules 21
Rosebury, Lord 30

St Cecilia's Hall 61
St Giles 43
St Giles Kirk 23, 39, 43, 44, 45, 48, 49
St John's Street 84, 85
St Mary's Street 73
Scottish Parliament 4, 13, 45, 95, 99, 100
Seafield, Earl of 87
Sempill's Close 13
Short, Maria 11
Sinclair, William 21
Smellie, William 52
Smith, Adam 51, 93
Smith, George 23, 24, 80
Smollet, Tobias 85
South Bridge 59
Stevenson, Robert Louis 24
Stewart, Dugald 93
Stewart, Sir James 37

Stewart. Margaret 67
Stripping Close 13
Surgeons' Square & Hall 75, 79

Tattoo, Edinburgh Military 4
Tollbooth 17, 19, 39, 40, 42
Town Guard 39, 40
Tron Kirk 47, 48, 57, 59, 88
Tweedale Court 69, 70

Victoria Street 17

Walker, Miss Nicky 56
Warriston Close 36, 38
Waverley Station 55
Weir, Major Thomas and Grizel 17, 18, 19
West Bow 4, 17, 19, 26, 40
White Horse Close 12, 97, 98
Wilson, Andrew 42
Wood, Dr. Alex 63
World's End Close 71
Writers' Museum 29

FURTHER READING

Arnot, Hugo: *The History of Edinburgh*
Birrell, J. F.: *An Edinburgh Alphabet*
Catford, F. E.: *Edinburgh. The Story of a City*
Chambers, Robert: *Traditions of Edinburgh*
Cockburn, Henry: *Memorials of his Time*
Coghill, Hamish: *Lost Edinburgh*
Cosh, Mary: *Edinburgh the Golden Age*
Dick, David: *Who was Who in the Royal Mile Edinburgh*
Grant, James: *Old and New Edinburgh*
Harris, Stuart: *The Place Names of Edinburgh*
Massie, Alan: *Edinburgh*
Melvin, Eric: *A Walk Through Edinburgh's New Town*
Ritchie, W. K.: *Edinburgh in the Golden Age*
Wilson, Sir Daniel: *Memorials of Edinburgh in the Olden Time*

Some of these titles are out of print. A good source for locating such titles is: www.abebooks.co.uk

The City of Edinburgh Council Libraries have an excellent site of illustrated material relating to Edinburgh at www.capitalcollections.com

ABOUT THE AUTHOR

Eric Melvin graduated with First Class Honours in History and Political Thought from Edinburgh University in 1967. He qualified as secondary teacher of History and Modern Studies. He retired from teaching in 2005, working latterly as Headteacher at Currie Community High School in Edinburgh.

In addition to teaching History at school, Eric has for many years taken Community Education classes for The City of Edinburgh Council in both Scottish History and The History of Edinburgh. He also give talks to various groups on aspects of the City's History. (e.g. Probus and Local History Clubs). Eric is a trained volunteer guide for The Edinburgh Festival Voluntary Guides Association and regularly takes groups down the Royal Mile and through the New Town

Eric has had several books published for younger readers on aspects of Scottish History and is the author of the companion volume *'A Walk Through Edinburgh's New Town'*. He is a member of the High Constables of Edinburgh, the historic bodyguard of Edinburgh's Lord Provost. He helps at the Oxfam Bookshop at Morningside and has done voluntary teaching at Chogoria Girls' High School in Kenya.

Eric is married to Lynda, a retired Nursery School Teacher. They have two sons, John, currently lecturing in Heritage Tourism at Hosei University in Tokyo, and Graeme, also working in Tokyo as a Business Communications Skills Trainer for American Express. John is married to Shizue Ichikawa from Sakata in Japan. They are the proud parents of Isla born in August 2010 and Rui born in April 2013.

Made in the USA
Charleston, SC
12 April 2016